# FOLKLORE AND LEGENDS of ROCHESTER

## THE MYSTERY OF HOODOO CORNER & OTHER TALES

MICHAEL T. KEENE

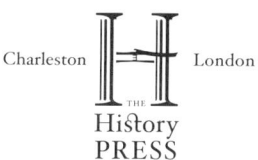

Published by The History Press
Charleston, SC 29403
www.historypress.net

Copyright © 2011 by Michael T. Keene
All rights reserved

*Illustrations courtesy of Ad-Hoc Productions.*

*Cover images courtesy of the Rochester Museum & Science Center and the Rochester Public Library.*

First published 2011

Manufactured in the United States

ISBN 978.1.60949.190.1

Library of Congress Cataloging-in-Publication Data

Keene, Michael.
Folklore and legends of Rochester : the mystery of Hoodoo Corner and other tales / Michael Keene.
p. cm.
Includes bibliographical references.
ISBN 978-1-60949-190-1
1. Folklore--New York (State)--Rochester. 2. Legends--New York (State)--Rochester. 3. Tales--New York (State)--Rochester. 4. Hoodoo (Cult)--New York (State)--Rochester. 5. Rochester (N.Y.)--Social life and customs--Anecdotes. 6. Rochester (N.Y.)--Biography--Anecdotes. I. Title.
GR110.N7K44 2011
398.209747'89--dc22
2011000881

*Notice*: The information in this book is true and complete to the best of our knowledge. It is offered without guarantee on the part of the author or The History Press. The author and The History Press disclaim all liability in connection with the use of this book.
All rights reserved. No part of this book may be reproduced or transmitted in any form whatsoever without prior written permission from the publisher except in the case of brief quotations embodied in critical articles and reviews.

# DEMOCRAT AND CHRONICLE

Rochester, N.Y., Saturday, January 27, 1931

### J.C. McCurdy, Department Store Founder, Dies at 81 After Illness of Four Years.

*Merchant Came to U.S. in Early 70's and Started Business Here in 1901*

An illness that forced his retirement from active business more than four years ago, yesterday resulted in the death of John C. McCurdy, founder of McCurdy's & Co., for many years one of the leading merchants in Rochester. He was 81.

Born near Londonderry, Ireland, June 26, 1852, the son of James and Jane Cooke McCurdy, Mr. McCurdy came to this country in the early [18]70's and settled in Philadelphia where for several years he and his brother James engaged in the operation of a department store. Closing out his Philadelphia business, Mr. McCurdy decided to move to another city and establish a new merchandising establishment. After investigating conditions in several Eastern cities, he moved to Rochester in March 1901, organized the McCurdy, Norwell Company and took over the present site of the McCurdy store at Main and Elm Streets.

Subsequent to Mr. McCurdy making his intentions known of desiring the Main and Elm Street property, he was approached by several area merchants who warned him that it was a legend in the trade marts that any enterprise started there was doomed to fail and quickly crash upon the shoals of destruction. What's more, this site was widely spoken of in those days as "hoodoo corner." [emphasis added]

# Contents

Introduction 7

1. Hoodoo Corner 9
2. Masters of the Crossroads 13
3. Hoodoo 18
4. The Code of Handsome Lake 26
5. The Psychic Highway 39
6. The Strange Disappearance of Captain William Morgan 49
7. Root Work 66
8. The Murder of William Lyman 80
9. Hoodoo Doctor 94
10. The Strange and Tragic Lives of the Fox Sisters 111

Conclusion: The Legend of Hoodoo Corner 133
Appendix: Hoodoo Corner Timeline 137
Notes 139
About the Author 143

# Introduction

I am not a professional historian or filmmaker, but I've always been a student of history and harbored a secret desire to produce films. Five years ago, I decided to see if I could turn my pipe dream into reality and try my hand at making a historical documentary. The subject matter I chose involved tracing the origins of a Rochester landmark, Midtown Plaza, located on the corner of Main and Elm Streets in downtown Rochester. I thought this would make for a good subject since I had parked my car in Midtown Plaza's underground parking garage for the past twenty years, across the street from where I worked and where I had frequented many of the plaza's shops and restaurants. In essence, this was a place I felt connected to and thought I knew a lot about. Little did I realize how much there was to learn or how Midtown Plaza and its history would come to dominate my thoughts for the next five years.

"Midtown," as it is now commonly called, holds the distinction of being the first urban indoor shopping center ever built in the United States. When it opened in 1962, it became national news, and because of its once-grand demeanor, it was, at the time, called "the vision that saved a city." But by the 1990s, it had a soaring vacancy rate and was in deteriorating physical shape; it was on the verge of closing. Its plight mirrored issues in many aging urban centers, and it seemed a timely subject for a story, especially since there was considerable local interest in its fate. As I set about exploring the history of Midtown, I soon become aware of a series of strange and remarkable true stories and historical characters that propelled me on a journey that continues to this day. As I learned the origins of Rochester's remarkable

## Introduction

history, including the founding of the modern spiritualist movement, the anti-Masonic movement, the supernatural visions of the Seneca Prophet Handsome Lake, the formation of the Mormon Church by Joseph Smith and the local connections to the abolitionist movement and the women's rights movement, I began to realize that the area now occupied by Midtown Plaza had been the epicenter of many of America's most important religious, social and political movements of the nineteenth century. But that's not where my journey started. It started with an unlikely source, a 1931 obituary of one of Rochester's most prominent businessmen who founded a local department store, and a curious reference to an area where the store was located, known as "Hoodoo Corner."

## CHAPTER 1
# Hoodoo Corner

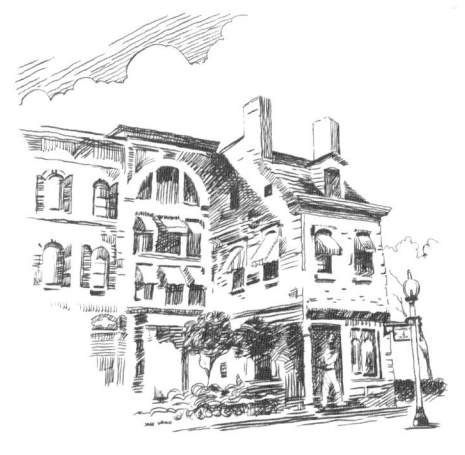

The modern history of Rochester's "Hoodoo Corner" (the intersection of Main and Elm Streets) as I came to know it, began in 1958, with a chance luncheon meeting by two leading merchants of the city: Gilbert J. McCurdy and Maurice Forman. Each owned a department store in the area, and largely due to the trend toward suburbanization that was then taking place in Rochester as well as across the United States, with its concomitant reliance on the automobile, they found themselves in need of more parking spaces for their customers. The men discussed the issue, which quickly became a broader conversation about revitalizing the entire midtown area. Thus the seeds were planted for a development that would change the face of Rochester.

A few months later, McCurdy had a heart attack. While he was in the hospital recovering, he happened on a newspaper article about the recently opened, first indoor shopping mall in the United States. He was so intrigued by the write-up that as soon as he was well enough, he went to Edina, Minnesota, to see it for himself. Southdale Mall was huge news when it opened: the two-story, 800,000-square-foot center contained space for seventy-two stores and two anchors and boasted 5,200 parking spaces. The mall officially opened on October 8, 1956, and had forty thousand visitors in the first day. It signaled the development of a new kind of retail destination that would spread across the country in the ensuing decades.

The $20 million project was developed by the Dayton Company, which had chosen a remarkable architect for the project. Victor Gruen (1903–1980), who would later become known as the "Mall-Maker," was a Jewish refugee from Hitler's Austria. In the summer of 1938, Gruen heard a knock on his door. Upon opening it, he was immediately arrested by Hitler's police, who confiscated his apartment, his business and his money. He was thrown into prison like many of the more prosperous Jews living in Vienna at the time. Eventually, he was released but saw the "writing on the wall" and left Vienna for America the same week as Sigmund Freud. Gruen carried with him a vision of community that would have profound—and some might say, paradoxical—consequences in his adopted country. He'd studied at the Technological Institute and Academy of Fine Arts in Vienna, the same institution to which Adolf Hitler was denied entry, and then worked for Peter Behrens before opening his own architecture firm in 1933. He was a committed socialist, an urban planner and a lover of the city.

He reportedly said upon landing in the United States in 1938: "I have nothing, but I am free." But it's not quite true that he had nothing. Though he spoke no English, had no place to live and no money, he had an architecture degree, a set of ideas and a network of contacts and friends that would prove invaluable. He soon began working as a draftsman in New York City. He became acquainted with the likes of George S. Kaufman, Richard Rodgers, Al Jolson, Irving Berlin and Albert Einstein. Gruen, who became a U.S. citizen in 1943, was by then already well on his way to making a name for himself. He was noticed by the architecture community, particularly for his innovative design for a Fifth Avenue leather goods shop, Lederer's. He incorporated a miniarcade into the design for the storefront and then into an original concept in retail design, one that would factor into much of his subsequent work. By 1951, he had moved to Los Angeles and founded his own firm, in which he brought together a talented group of architects, engineers and planners.[1]

As one critic noted in a review of Victor Gruen's book, *The Heart of Our Cities*, he was "anxious to work towards an ideal city, the perfect man-made environment."[2] Gruen arguably imported this tendency with him when he emigrated from Vienna, which had undergone a dramatic reconstruction since the late nineteenth century, when the fortifications around the city were demolished. The new city was laid out quite deliberately, in response to larger political and civic ideas about the ways in which residents from different classes should mingle as they moved through an urban area. It became a central organizing principle of Gruen's work as well, and he would bring it to both his urban master plans for cities like Fort Worth, Kalamazoo and Cincinnati, as well as the mall designs he pioneered in cities like Detroit, Edina, Philadelphia and Rochester. In all, Gruen was involved in the development of some two hundred malls across the United States.

His first enclosed shopping mall, Southdale, incorporated elements that would become nearly universal in malls across the country: everything was under one roof, with heating and air conditioning to protect shoppers from the elements; it was built on two levels to reduce walking; and it had escalators at the ends of aisles to encourage shoppers to stroll past every store before changing direction. The mall contained a kind of town square in the center, with a restaurant, skylight and a parklike setting. But Gruen did not envision Southdale as solely a retail destination. The initial master plan, which was never fully realized, was an entire development that included apartments, houses, schools and parks. The mall was designed to meet leisure and practical needs and to serve as a community gathering place. It included space for a post office, a grocery store and even a small zoo, among other things. Gruen aimed to create an aesthetically pleasing as well as functional space, including artwork, decorative lighting, fountains and tropical plants and flowers.

The opening of the mall was covered by media nationwide, which is what drew McCurdy's attention to it. And he was impressed enough by the design of Southdale that, after his visit to it, he sought out Gruen, and the two began discussing a suitable project for Rochester. Such a project accorded with Gruen's notion of a mall as the centerpiece of a carefully planned downtown; he signed on.

Then McCurdy took a lesson from another visionary of the period. He soon engaged the services of real estate attorney Wallace "Bud" Weiser, and the two, copying Walt Disney's approach to acquiring the property on which he built Disney World (that is, not advertising their intentions, so as not to drive up the cost of the targeted real estate parcels), began quietly buying up the required land. In eighteen months, they had acquired eighteen separate parcels along Elm and Main Streets in Rochester.

McCurdy's plans for the property were soon approved by the Rochester City Council, and construction began in 1960. The plans for the shopping center included a fifteen-story hotel, retail space and a 1,900-space underground parking garage. It was the single largest private investment in

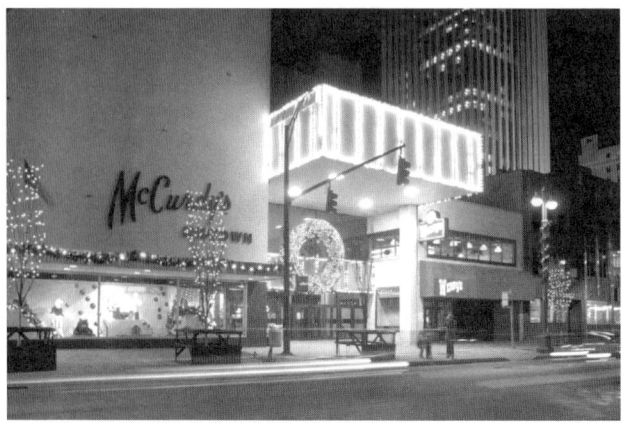

Midtown Plaza opens in 1962 as the first indoor urban shopping center in the United States. Its location includes the intersection of Main and Elm Streets. *Courtesy of Rochester Museum & Science Center.*

retailing in the United States at that time. On April 10, 1962, Midtown Plaza was dedicated. Over seven thousand people attended opening-day festivities. National media covered the event, including a story on the *Huntley-Brinkley Report*, NBC's nightly national newscast. The opening of Midtown Plaza was hailed locally as a "vision that saved a city" and a "Renaissance on the Genesee." Even Walt Disney himself eventually visited the property.

By the end of his life, Victor Gruen had largely changed his mind about the role of shopping malls in American life, and he even disavowed the form he had pioneered. He was quite disillusioned by the sprawling developments that grew up around many of the malls he had built. In 1978, just two years before he died—back in his native Austria, where he had moved in the late 1960s, living in a country house just outside Vienna—he gave a speech in which he railed against American suburban life, of which his malls were an integral part, calling them "avenues of horror, flanked by the greatest collection of vulgarity—billboards, motels, gas stations, shanties, car lots, miscellaneous industrial equipment, hot dog stands, wayside stores—ever collected by mankind."[3]

And Midtown Plaza, by the early 1990s, reflected the ways in which these developments had come together. In the course of the late twentieth century, retailing had become largely a suburban phenomenon, depriving cities of one of their main economic engines. Gruen's shopping mall in the heart of Rochester had become a symbol of urban decay: it was now as out of fashion as the family-owned department stores that had previously been located at that intersection. So intrigued as I was by the men who were instrumental in the making of Midtown Plaza and the historical developments that led to its creation, I turned my attention further back in history to better understand the dynamics of the origins of Midtown Plaza and to a legend known as Hoodoo Corner.

## CHAPTER 2
# Masters of the Crossroads

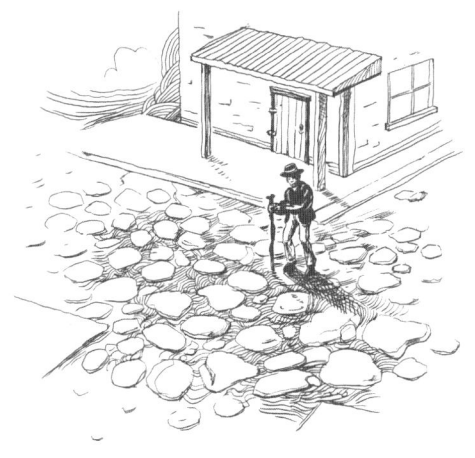

Benjamin Forman, whose son Maurice had that pivotal lunch with McCurdy, moved in the late nineteenth century to America from his home near the Russian-Austrian border. He found himself in New York City at age eighteen, and he worked in the garment district as a tailor. Eventually he decided to strike out on his own and moved to Ithaca, New York, where he toiled as an itinerant tailor, going door-to-door with a pack filled with cloth, needles and thread. He became well known for his skill with women's wear, and when he arrived in Rochester in 1912, he founded B. Forman's. The store quickly developed a reputation as the finest purveyor of women's clothing between New York City and Chicago. Forman's also became well known as a training ground for retailers and as the "incubator of CEOs," as it trained many men who went on to play key roles in the development of retailers like Federated, May and Abraham Strauss. Benjamin Forman was also particularly well known for an eccentricity: it was said that he always carried a thimble in his suit pocket, in remembrance of his humble beginnings.

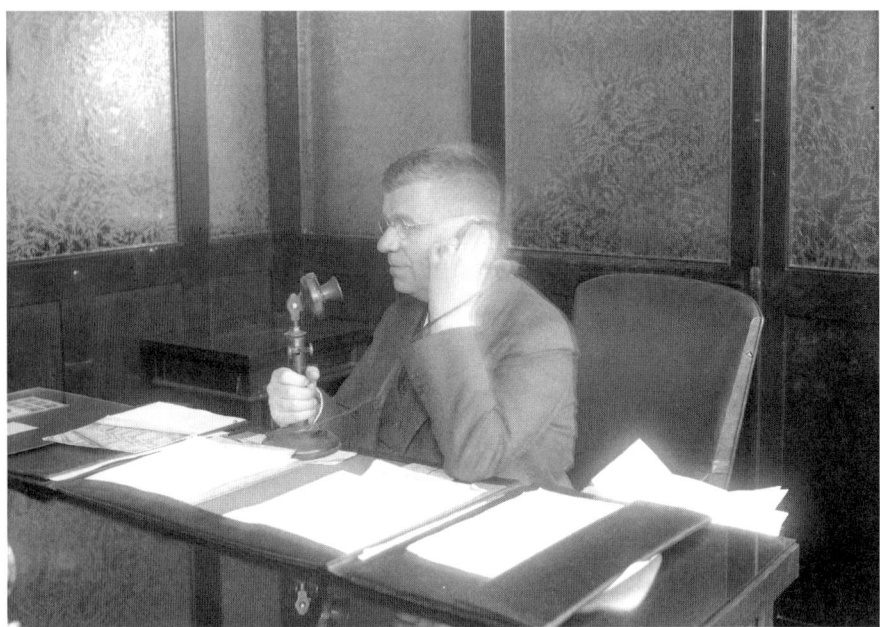

Benjamin Forman, 1875–1953, itinerant peddler of cloth, needles and thread, went on to become founder of B. Forman's. *Courtesy of Rochester Museum & Science Center.*

John C. McCurdy, the father of Gilbert McCurdy, was the founder of the other department store that was located at Main and Elm Streets. The elder McCurdy, born into a family of Belfast grocers, had emigrated from Ireland in the 1870s and settled in Philadelphia, where he and his brother ran a department store. Eventually, the McCurdy brothers sold that concern, and John, determined to try his luck elsewhere, traveled around the eastern United States, looking for a promising location. He finally settled on Rochester, and in 1901, he relocated to the city.

McCurdy had determined that Main and Elm Streets was the geographical center of retailing in the city, and it was thus the best place to pursue a business. There was an existing store at the location: Carroll's Department Store. McCurdy bought the store, lock, stock and barrel, and renamed it the McCurdy & Norwell Company. At its peak, the store employed five hundred people. It would remain in the McCurdy family for the next ninety years.

Befitting his stature in the community, when John C. McCurdy died in 1931, his obituary was carried on the front page of the local paper, the *Democrat Chronicle*. One paragraph in the article particularly caught my attention: when McCurdy was exploring the possibility of buying Carroll's, it was reported, he

# Masters of the Crossroads

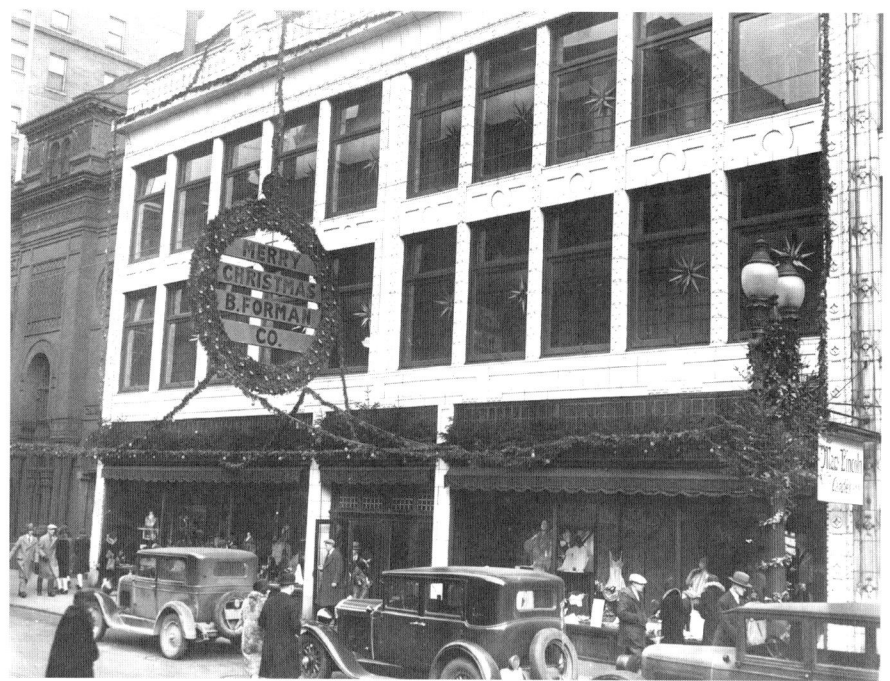

B. Forman's was established in 1908 and was considered the finest women's clothing store between New York and Chicago. It became an important anchor of Midtown Plaza. *Courtesy of Rochester Museum & Science Center.*

was warned against it by a number of neighboring merchants. The reporter explained that "the site was spoken of in those days as 'Hoodoo Corner' and it was a legend in the trade marts that all enterprises started there quickly came upon the shoals of destruction."[4] The reporter noted that McCurdy was "undaunted" by this superstition and went ahead with his plans anyway, and as history indicates, he became successful in every way.

But I found myself immediately intrigued by the term Hoodoo Corner, as well as by the idea that the area in which Midtown Plaza is now located might carry some kind of curse. I had never heard the term "hoodoo" before, and I'd lived in the city and worked in that precise area for many years. When I looked up the word in the dictionary, I found a list of definitions, none of which seemed necessarily related to one another or to Rochester. This is not so remarkable, perhaps—it often seems the case with dictionary entries, that the precise meaning or usage of a term in a particular instance lies just vaguely between the listed definitions or in some combination of them. I would find that this is particularly true in this case.

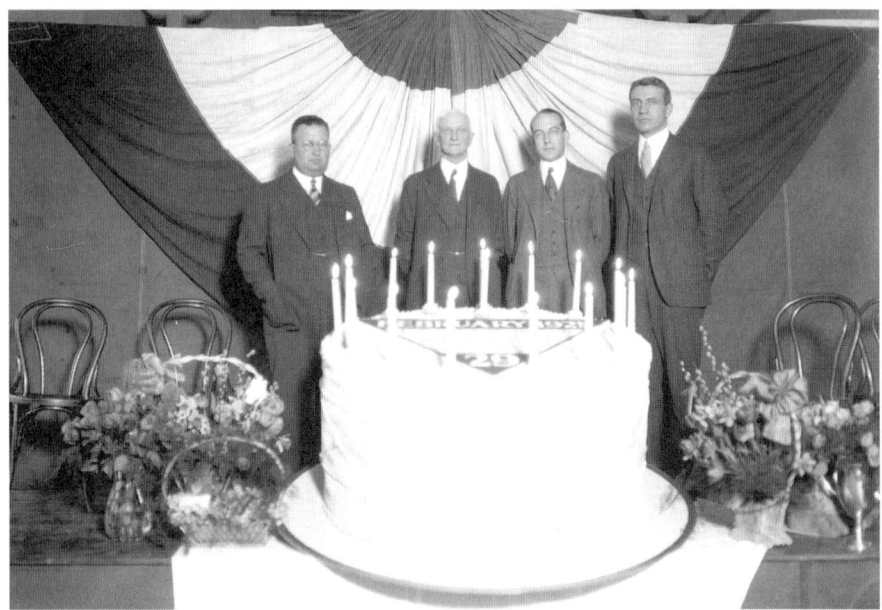

Gilbert McCurdy, 1895–1983, standing on far right, was instrumental in the development of Midtown Plaza. *Courtesy of Rochester Public Library.*

Thus would begin five years of research in attempting locate the origins of the Hoodoo Corner legend, and I found myself swept along from one historical episode to another, always going deeper into the material. I moved back and forth from secondary research (reading works on the history and culture of the region) to primary research (reading the original source documents in archives and libraries) to what might be called first-person research (traveling around Rochester and surrounding areas to see many of the sites of these events with my own eyes).

As I got to know the history of this region, I found myself getting to know the history of America. To a remarkable extent, the world we live in today can be traced to developments in the early nineteenth century, many of which took place in the area described as a sliver of land not more than twenty miles wide and twenty miles long located around Rochester. It was, for instance, the home of many key figures of the period, including Frederick Douglass, Susan B. Anthony and Joseph Smith, and of the founding of the country's great social, religious and political movements, such as the women's rights, abolitionist and anti-Masonic movements. But it was also home to a number of lesser-known historical figures, such as the Fox Sisters, Captain William Morgan, Handsome Lake, Thurlow Weed and many others who

## Masters of the Crossroads

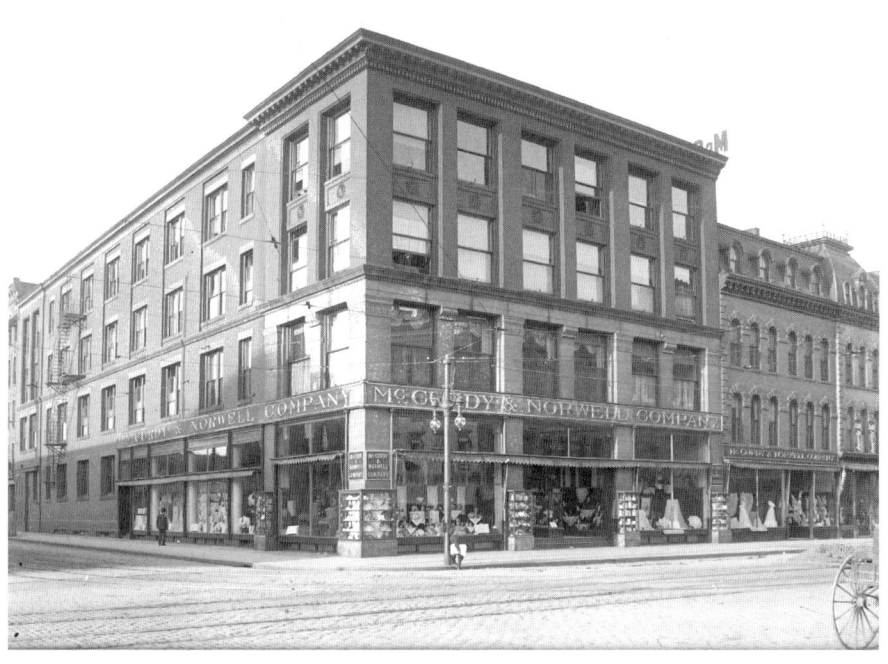

John C. McCurdy, 1858–1931, established McCurdy & Norwell Company. McCurdy was warned that the intersection of Main and Elm, known as Hoodoo Corner, was considered cursed. *Courtesy of Rochester Public Library.*

would go on to play crucial roles in the spiritual renaissance then taking place in America.

It was during this period, in particular, that religious and spiritual life in America became, in some senses, truly American. And in keeping with the general development of American history, the sources of these movements were a diverse collection of people, traditions and ideas: European immigrants, Native Americans and African Americans who all made lasting and significant contributions and almost all having a strange and powerful connection to a place known as Hoodoo Corner.

# CHAPTER 3
# Hoodoo

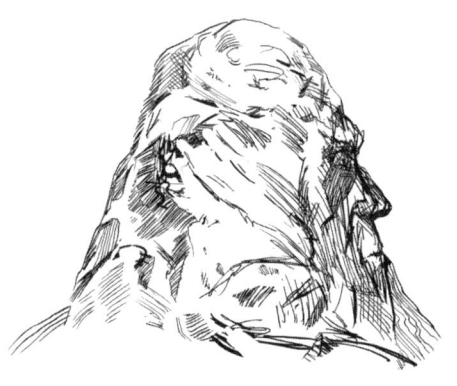

In most dictionaries, the hoodoo entry is a combination of four basic definitions along the following lines: 1) a geologic formation of rocks, especially a natural column of rock formed by weathering, often in fantastic shapes; 2) a folkloric magical practice, especially among African Americans in the south; 3) something that brings bad luck; and 4) foretelling the future.

Clearly, as I originally thought, the reference to Hoodoo Corner in the newspaper account of McCurdy's death carried the last meaning—the connotation of bad luck, a jinx—but that still left the much larger and more interesting question of why this particular corner in Rochester would be believed to carry a curse. The first two definitions did not seem, at first glance, to apply. Rochester is not, of course, in the American south, and the center of the city boasts no dramatic geological formations.

But I would find, as I researched the meaning of hoodoo, there is no one simple answer as to why it became associated with a corner in downtown Rochester. The answer, I would eventually discover, is an amalgamation of these concepts, a legend grown up through a series of historical events,

# Hoodoo

an accretion of meaning deposited by layers of time that can only be understood by examining these things in turn. In the end, of course, this means that the answer is necessarily speculative, but that doesn't mean it is untrue, and pursuing it offers numerous rewards and insights into our past. First, one cannot help but be reminded that the period of time in which the city of Rochester has existed is but the blink of an eye, just a few hundred years. Europeans began arriving in the area that would become Rochester in the late seventeenth century, though there is intriguing evidence that those who inhabited the area long before Europeans arrived may have attributed particular significance to the location that would become Hoodoo Corner.

Geologic evidence suggests that many millions of years ago, the upstate New York area was covered by a warm, shallow inland sea. Then, roughly a million years ago, the earth cooled dramatically, ushering in the Ice Age. The area that would one day include Rochester was covered four times with polar ice, with glaciers that were up to 2 miles thick. The glaciers acted like sandpaper on the landscape. Thus, vast areas in Canada were scraped down to bedrock, and the soil was pushed south, covering some areas of the Genesee Valley in glacial till up to three hundred feet deep. The glaciers also smoothed out ridges and rounded hills, allowing the formation of the lakes

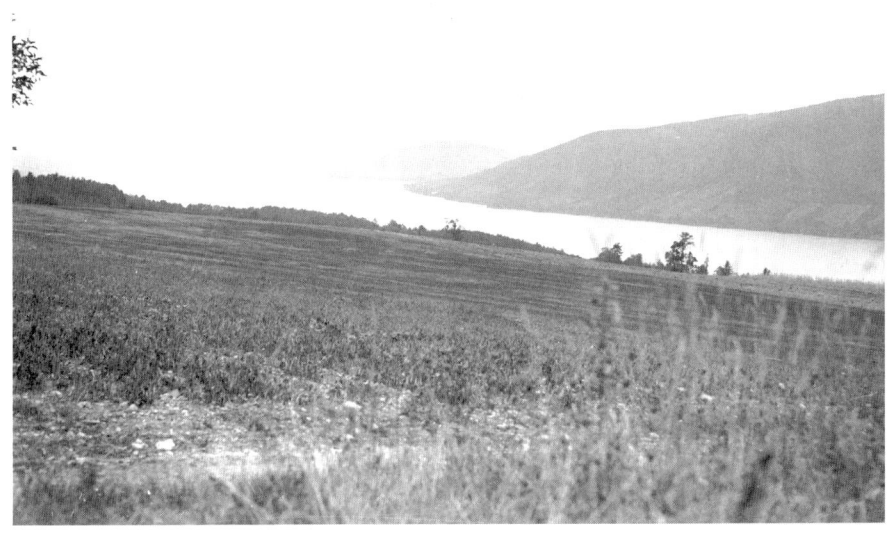

The Ice Age ends, and the great glaciers recede. Many geological formations are created, including the Finger Lakes, as well as phenomena of ice mountains called ice hoodoos. *Courtesy of Rochester Public Library.*

and many other geological formations, such as tent rocks, ice pyramids and, yes, even hoodoos. The fertile soil deposited by the glaciers would give rise to a rich and varied plant life, which eventually provided the habitat for varied animal life. Roughly half a million years ago, a gigantic sandbar started to form in one of these ancient lakes. The sandbar—extending 150 miles from present-day Sodus to Lewiston—formed a ridge that the first human inhabitants used as a primary east–west trail. And when Europeans began settling the area, they, too, made use of the trail: stagecoach lines followed the same ridge from 1818 to 1848. Today, New York State Route 104 follows the same geologic formation.

The earliest inhabitants of the region are believed to have been the Archaic Algonquians. They were a nomadic people, hunting and fishing in small groups. Archaeological evidence, such as knives and other implements, suggests that Inuit wandered the area as well. And there is substantial, intriguing evidence of other peoples inhabiting the area from 3,000 BCE through perhaps as late as the sixteenth century, though very little is known about them. They have been termed the Mound Builders, in reference to their practice of constructing earthen mounds for burial, ceremonial and residential purposes. There is also evidence to suggest that Native Americans who later migrated into the area availed themselves of the improvements left by the Mound Builders.

At any rate, historical and archaeological evidence suggests that modern Native Americans began moving to the area in the fourteenth century, migrating from the Ohio River Valley and the lower St. Lawrence area, though the tribal origin of these groups is not clear. We do know, however, that when Europeans began arriving in the area in the seventeenth century, Seneca Indians were in residence. The Seneca were one of the most powerful and warlike tribes of the Iroquois Nation, and they had widely settled the area between the Genesee River and Seneca Lake. Our earliest written sources on this topic, therefore, result from the contacts between Europeans and Indians.

Interestingly, the Seneca—who ascribed their own origins to a mountain at the head of Canandaigua Lake, which, oral tradition held, broke open and released the tribe—were well aware of the presence of the Mound Builders before them. According to the Seneca, their predecessors were a large people who were civil, industrious and enterprising. Tradition held that the Mound Builders had been "totally destroyed by the great serpent," leaving the Seneca to take possession of the improvements that had been left. Seneca legends about the Mound Builders' presence were sometimes

# Hoodoo

supported in quite dramatic ways: in 1796, for instance, a section of high bluff overlooking Irondequoit Bay caved off, exposing a "great quantity" of human bones. The skeletons, when reassembled, indicated a race "much taller and heavier" than either the Seneca or the Europeans. Some distance away, another skeleton that was unearthed during an excavation project proved to be nearly eight feet tall. The individual had been buried with copper pots and other implements.

Much of what is known about the Seneca in the area was gathered by early European settlers and citizens of the young republic, many of whom became amateur ethnographers and historians. One of the most valued contributions is that of George H. Harris (1843–1893), a descendant of early pioneers in the region. He was a lifelong student of the geography and history of the upstate New York area. And from the moment he found an Indian spearhead as a young boy, he was fascinated by the Seneca.

Harris's unique access to them was secured when, as a young teen, he saved the life of the son of Tall Chief. The young Seneca and a couple of other children were in a canoe on a river swollen with spring floods when they lost their paddles. Harris, who happened to be walking along the riverbank,

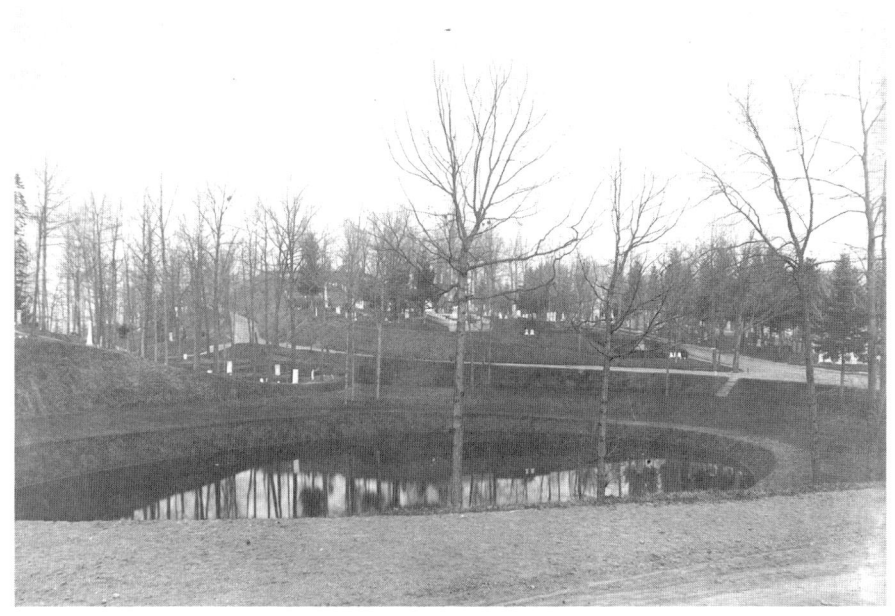

Sylvan Waters of Mount Hope Cemetery displays an example of an Ice Age creation, a glacial kettle. *Courtesy of Rochester Public Library.*

spotted the out-of-control canoe being pulled along by the current, headed for falls ahead. He ran ahead of it down the riverbank, grabbed some fishing lines he happened to have previously set and threw them to the canoe. He and the children worked to guide the canoe safely to shore, thus saving them from near-certain death. Tall Chief visited Harris's home shortly thereafter to thank him. A friendship of sorts was formed, and from then on, Harris regularly visited Tall Chief's encampment at Irondequoit Bay. Harris learned the Seneca language and absorbed their customs. Throughout his adult life, he continued to amass oral histories as well as conduct frequent geographical and archaeological surveys in the area, collecting numerous artifacts and relics. In 1889, he was made an honorary member of the Wolf clan. He was given the name Ho-tar-shan-nyoh, or Pathfinder.

It is an apt epithet, as Harris was trained in surveying and drafting as well as landscape gardening. He used his well-trained topographical eye and empathy for Native Americans in developing an appreciation of their way of life, especially the ways they adapted to the geography in which they lived. Harris produced a body of work that is notable both for its attention to detail and its even-handed approach to the indigenous population.

Harris sketched out—in words and maps—the main trails of the Iroquois. For our purposes, the most significant information is that the main trails converged on the Genesee in the vicinity of Rochester at two places: the ridge north of the lower falls and the rapids some five hundred yards below the mouth of Red Creek. The trail coming west from Canandaigua divided a few rods east of Allen's creek, with the westward trail tracing the route that would one day become East Avenue. This particular branch crossed Main Street and struck the river trail in the vicinity of Franklin and North St. Paul Streets. Incredibly, the intersection that came to be called Hoodoo Corner was originally an intersection of Native American trails long before it was an intersection of streets. Numerous sources suggest that there was an Indian burial ground nearby, which may have been designated with rock piles. Because it is common to find the term hoodoo attached to former Indian lands in other areas of the country, especially to areas that seemed to be of critical importance to the Indians, it is possible that this is the basis of the term becoming attached to this area. In other words, Hoodoo Corner may have once been an ancient burial ground.

And the term hoodoo is interesting in this respect—though also tricky—because it has shades of meaning that attach to its various definitions. The connotation, in other words, is frequently negative, and it seems to become

# Hoodoo

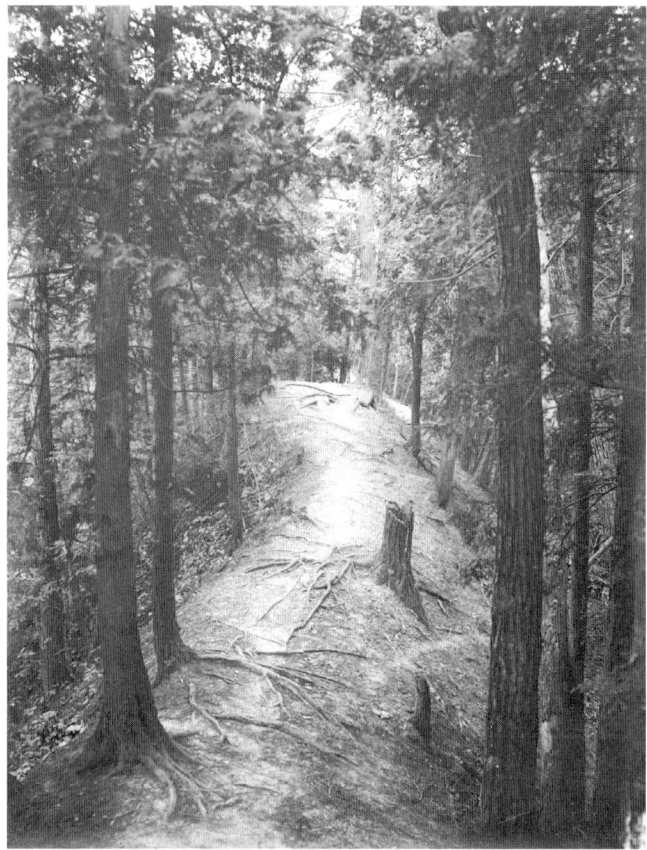

The Indian trail that would later become East Avenue. The trail ended near Main and Elm Streets, the site of a Seneca cemetery marked by a man-made hoodoo. *Courtesy of Rochester Museum & Science Center.*

more negative the further one gets from the geologic definition. This is in part due to misapprehension of Native American religion and culture on the part of European settlers, as well as the bloody history of relations between the two groups. And it may be significant that the area around Rochester, and Hoodoo Corner, was a primary arena in the struggle between the two groups.

The first non–Native American settler in the Rochester area was Ebenezer "Indian" Allan (circa 1753–1813).[5] Little is known about his early life—even his exact birth date and birthplace is not known for sure—though it is believed that he was born and raised in New Jersey. He is a complicated, controversial and colorful figure, and it is difficult to separate legend from fact when reconstructing his life. As one commentator notes, "no Western New Yorker was ever more heartily despised by his neighbors." Another called him the "bad boy of the Genesee." He was known as shrewd, unscrupulous, lawless and brutal. He was also known as a soldier, polygamist, farmer, miller and especially as a trader, dealmaker and sometimes peacemaker with the Seneca. He may have been a murderer as well.[6]

By the late 1780s, Allan lived in the Genesee Valley region, where he distinguished himself from his neighbors in both his personal and professional life. His ideas about marriage were particularly out of step with his time, not only because he practiced polygamy, but because he chose nonwhite partners. His first Indian companion was a woman named Sally, who eventually bore him two daughters. They built a cabin and set up a homestead, in what is now Scottsville, on land either bought or given to him by the Seneca. He earned a living by farming, raising stock and trading with the Indians.

And perhaps because of his familiarity with the Seneca, Indian Allan was brought into a historic land deal, the ethics of which are still disputed by historians. In 1788, Oliver Phelps and Nathaniel Gorham purchased from the State of Massachusetts some 6 million acres of land in western New York. But a large portion of this land was under Indian title. Phelps and Gorham set about extinguishing Indian title to land west of the Genesee and, to this end, undertook complicated negotiations with the Buffalo Creek Indian Council. The historical record suggests that Phelps behaved unethically in the negotiations: preying on the Indians' economic need—and naiveté about the amount of land required for a construction project—he acquired some 288 square miles of land adjacent to the Genesee River for no more than a promise to build a gristmill there for the use of the Iroquois.

Phelps turned to Allan, giving him a one-hundred-acre tract with the understanding that Allan would build and run the mill. The parcel was located near a waterfall to provide power for turning the stones. Allan and fourteen men raised the building by the summer of 1789. Those one hundred acres were the nucleus of Rochester, and this gristmill was its first construction project. (It was located on the south side of present-day Race Street, between Aqueduct and Graves Streets.) The end of construction was celebrated with a party that lasted two days, fueled by a keg of rum that had been dropped by a trading vessel.[7]

Within two years, Allan had sold the mill and moved to Mount Morris, after having acquired at least one more wife, Millie Gregory, who would eventually bear him six children. There were rumors as well that he had taken perhaps one or two more Indian wives, at least one of which he reportedly tried to have murdered. Allan eventually moved to Canada and died there in 1813.

Hoodoo

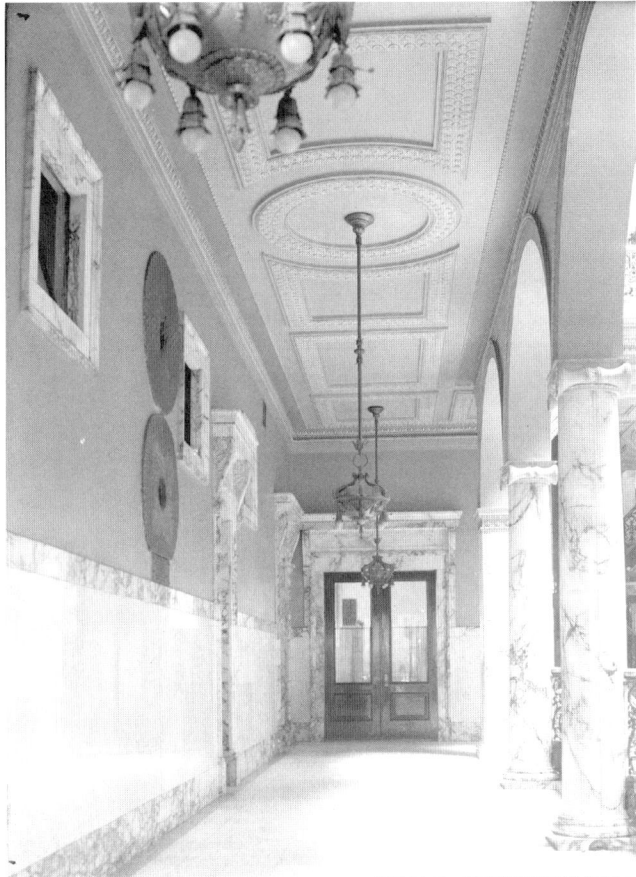

Hallway containing a plaque commemorates Ebenezer "Indian" Allan's gristmill. He was the first white settler in Rochester, and it's believed that he murdered two of his wives. *Courtesy of Rochester Museum & Science Center.*

Even though Allan's gristmill proved to be an economic failure, it did have the virtue of offering a vision for those future explorers who would ultimately be successful in exploiting the region's natural resources. But it is the life of another visionary we must now visit, a leader whose supernatural visions would be credited with saving a people and their culture, and whose journey would intersect with Hoodoo Corner.

# CHAPTER 4
# The Code of Handsome Lake

In early June 1799, a young Seneca woman sat outside the door of her family's home. She was waiting for her father to die. He had been sick for nearly four years and was now little but "yellow skin and dried bones." Suddenly, she heard him call out "*Nüo*," and then he burst out the door. He swayed, and she 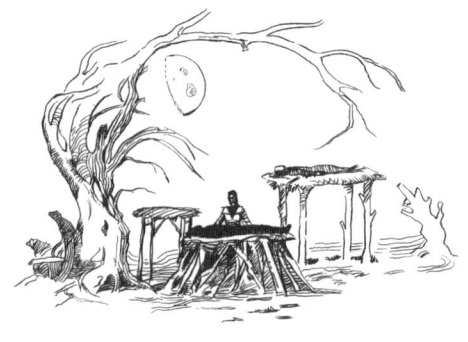 stood quickly to catch him as he fell into her arms. She took him back to his bed. Then she dressed him in burial clothes and sent for his closest male relatives, Blacksnake and Cornplanter. By the time they arrived, it appeared that the old man was dead: there was no breathing, no heartbeat, and the body was cool to the touch.

But the man wasn't dead. Blacksnake soon discovered a warm spot on the sick man's chest. Then the man began breathing again. The warm spot grew bigger and bigger, as if life was returning to the man's body bit by bit. After two hours, the man finally opened his eyes and began to speak. He described a journey he had taken while he lay there, unconscious. In this vision, he met with messengers who spoke to him of the problems of his people, and the proper way to deal with them. No one knew it yet, but the journey the man took while he lay there, somewhere between life and death,

# The Code of Handsome Lake

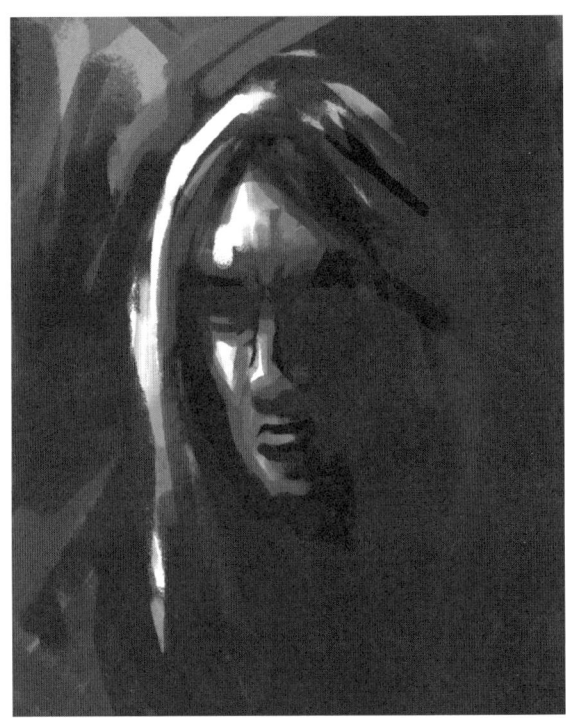

An illustration of Seneca prophet Handsome Lake, 1745–1815. After nearly dying of alcoholism, he became a significant moral leader.

was the first of a series of visitations he would have from the messengers. They would inspire, over the sixteen years the man had remaining to him, an entire philosophy—a code of life and conduct—that would change the historical course of his people. In the end, Handsome Lake would become known as a great prophet and the savior of the Seneca Nation.

\* \* \*

Handsome Lake (circa 1735–1815) was born Hadawa'ko (Shaking Snow) in the Seneca village of Conewaugus, located on the Genesee River near present-day Avon. Very little is known of his parents or his early life. He was born into the Wolf clan, although he was eventually raised by the Turtle clan.

When he was born, the Seneca—indeed, the entire Iroquois Confederacy—was at the height of its power and prosperity. But the fortunes of the Indians fell precipitously during the eighteenth century, and over the course of his life, Handsome Lake would be both witness to and victim of this social and cultural decline. It is fair to say that the summer afternoon when Handsome Lake lay apparently dying was the lowest point of his life and, perhaps, that of the life of his people as well.

The Iroquois Confederacy had continuously existed since the fourteenth century. Its constitution—the Great Law of Peace, an orally transmitted document—is one of the oldest constitutions in the world. It described a federal union of five (later six) Indian nations: Mohawk, Onondaga, Seneca, Oneida, Cayuga and Tuscarora. The document (which was finally put into writing in 1915 by Arthur C. Parker, an archaeologist and Indian specialist who worked for the State Museum of New York) is often mentioned along with the likes of the Magna Carta in terms of the greatest political documents in history.

It provided a framework for working out problems among the nations' members and described political and social systems that were balanced and largely egalitarian. Iroquois society was matrilineal, meaning that land ownership and ancestry were determined by tracing heritage through the mother's line. The Iroquois are sometimes referred to as "the people of the longhouse," the translation from the nation's own word (*haudenosaunee*) for itself. (The word "Iroquois" is an appellation of French missionaries and represents the way they heard the term *hiro kone*, meaning "I have spoken." It was a ritual expression with which Iroquois typically ended their orations). The tribe's term for itself is based on its primary form of social and family organization: the longhouse. Ranging from twenty-five to four hundred feet long, these narrow, rectangular structures housed entire clans, traced along the maternal line. The longhouses were divided into compartments, with a long central hall. Each family had its own personal space of about six feet by nine feet. The structure typically held twenty or more families. Each clan had its own name, typically an animal name.

There was no "state" religion—each tribe was free to celebrate its own religious rites and festivals. Civil affairs were separate from religious affairs. This is not to suggest that there was an Iroquois idyll before first contact with the Europeans. Rather, the Iroquois had a highly developed, highly functional political and social system that would be shattered by its intersection with the founding of the new American nation.

Initial contacts between Europeans and the Iroquois were generally positive, and relations remained friendly and respectful through the mid-eighteenth century. Though our Thanksgiving notions of Native Americans and white settlers sitting down to celebrate the fall harvest with a meal

# The Code of Handsome Lake

(complete with a cornucopia on the table) may be somewhat simplistic, there is a kernel of truth in that image. Many settlers relied on trade with the Indians for survival and freely adopted those Indian customs, ideas and modes of living that made adaptation to the New World easier.

During the colonial era, Indian leaders and statesmen met as equals to diplomatically solve problems. Good trade relationships were critical to the prosperity of the colonies, and this provided powerful incentives to alleviate strains in relations. Many early Americans also plainly admired the Indians. For instance, Benjamin Franklin, who served as an Indian commissioner, studied the Indian way of life, published accounts of treaty negotiations and cited the Iroquois model in his arguments about relations between the British and the colonies. Franklin stressed the fact that the individual nations of the confederacy managed their own internal affairs without interference from the Grand Council.

Other founding fathers like Thomas Jefferson, John Adams and George Washington were familiar with and admired the Iroquois' federal form of government. Each nation was represented at the Confederate Council by one political leader and one war leader. The confederacy included a system of checks and balances, with each nation holding veto power for certain

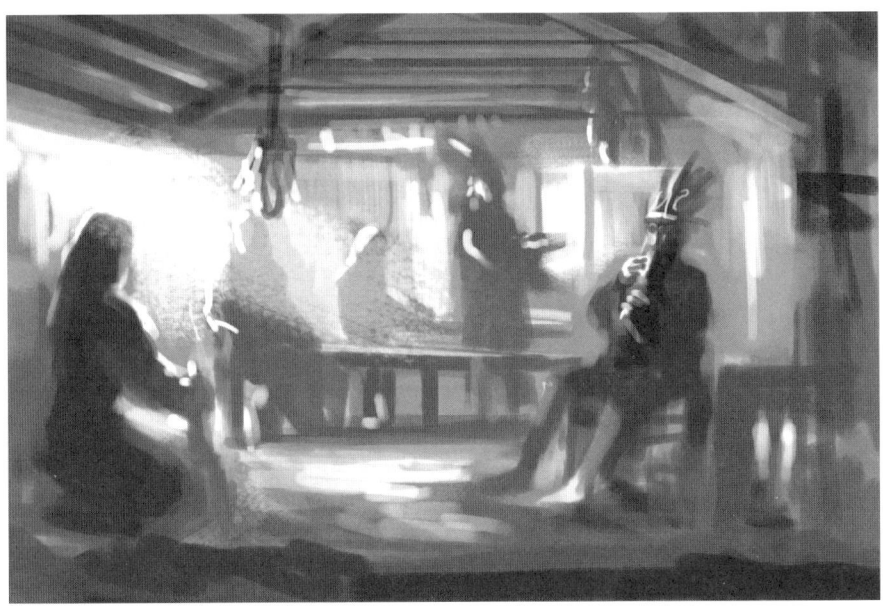

An illustration of a Seneca Council house, as depicted in the documentary *The Code of Handsome Lake*.

actions. Each individual nation had a system for choosing its leaders, and there were impeachment provisions as well, ensuring that leaders governed in accordance with public consent. Much of this should be familiar to Americans and for good reason: historians have shown that the federal system of the U.S. government and the U.S. Constitution was patterned in part on the Iroquois system.[8]

But the Iroquois system underwent a severe challenge with the outbreak of the American Revolution. Both the British and the Americans sought the allegiance—or at least the neutrality—of the Iroquois Confederacy. The six nations divided: most Mohawk, Cayuga, Onondaga and Seneca tribes chose to ally with the British, while most Oneida and Tuscarora tribes joined the American revolutionaries. In some sense, the American Revolution became a civil war for the Iroquois, and the divisions that precipitated the split would grow wider during the years of war and go on to echo in internal Indian debates in the ensuing decades.

In particular, the results of the War of Independence would be disastrous for the Seneca, who not only chose the losing side but stuck with it until the end. For instance, even after the British surrender at Saratoga, Loyalists and their Iroquois allies in upper New York continued to raid American settlements as well as the villages of fellow Iroquois who had been allied with the revolutionaries. Seneca chief Cornplanter led some of these raids, alongside Loyalist commanders, such as John Butler (with whom Indian Allan served).

In 1777, the Continental Congress, concerned that a major Indian war was imminent, decided to raise an army of three thousand men to deal with the Indian problem on the frontier. Planning and preparations were slow, and it would take roughly another year to be brought to fruition. But the course of events during that year only hardened the resolve of the Americans. Indian-Loyalist attacks on settlers continued. There were some reprisals by American units already in the field, but the small number of available troops made it nearly impossible to offer an effective defense or to thwart the ability of the Indians and Loyalists to mount attacks.

The turning point was a major Iroquois raid in November 1778, when nearly four hundred Indians, led by Cornplanter, launched an assault on a fort near Cherry Valley. The so-called Cherry Valley Massacre—in which approximately fifty soldiers and civilians died, with another eighty taken captive—forced the hand of the fledgling American government. General George Washington assigned Major General John Sullivan to lead the new force to deal with the Seneca.

# The Code of Handsome Lake

The Sullivan Expedition, as this campaign would come to be known, was notorious for the toll it took on both sides. In the end, Colonel Sullivan had nearly four thousand men at his command, and he drove them and their horses tirelessly. The village of Horseheads, in the southern tier of New York, acquired its name from an event during this campaign: the pack horses of Sullivan's army, having hauled heavy military equipment for over four hundred miles through difficult terrain, reached the end of their endurance in a little valley, and there the horses were slaughtered en masse. A few years later, horse skulls were arrayed along the trail by returning Native Americans, reportedly as a warning or as a gesture of anger or defiance.

* * *

The devastation of the Sullivan Expedition created great hardship for more than five thousand Iroquois refugees the following winter, and many starved or froze to death. And although General Washington was disappointed by what he perceived as the lack of a clear military verdict—there was only one major battle during the campaign—it nevertheless became clear in the long term that the victory of the new American nation over the Iroquois was complete. The infrastructure of the Iroquois Confederacy had been devastated. But the damage was much deeper and lasted longer than physical losses. In the final analysis, the significance of the Sullivan Expedition is that it broke not only the means of the Iroquois Confederacy to defend its territory by making war but its very will to do so. And as his nation's will was broken, so was that of Handsome Lake. He, like so many of his compatriots, gave in to despair and to alcoholism.

Over the next decade, a series of treaties—with their predictable ex-post-facto claims and counterclaims—were executed, and while some small groups of Iroquois were moved onto reservations in the region, many more were moved to reservations in Canada and beyond the American frontier (which then meant west and north of Illinois, essentially). After the Treaty of Paris was signed in 1783—formally ending the war between the British and the Americans—white settlers began moving west into New York, areas made safe by the removal of Indians.

All of this led to critical issues for the Seneca, especially given the grim conditions on the reservations. The standard of living was abysmal, and there was rampant cultural and social breakdown: alcoholism, domestic abuse and shattered families. There were accusations of witchcraft, as is so often the case in such conditions. Iroquois social structure was crumbling under reservation life, and traditional religious practices were insufficient to meet the needs of the people. Until that summer day in 1799, it is perhaps fair to say that Handsome Lake had been as much a victim of these conditions as any other Seneca.

There is mysteriously (and frustratingly) little known about Handsome Lake's life prior to his near-death experience and the visions that accompanied it. He was described by Buffalo Tom Jemison as a middle-sized man, slim and unhealthy looking. He was a member of a noble family, though nothing is known about them (other than Cornplanter and Red Jacket). Handsome Lake's warrior name is unknown, as is the provenance of the name under which we know him. His name does appear on a 1794 treaty, but what role he might have played in the negotiations is unknown.

It is known, however, that after the loss of the bulk of Seneca lands in the Genesee area, he went with members of his tribe to settlements on the Allegheny River. By many accounts, he was an alcoholic for some twenty years—and quite seriously ill, perhaps with the complications that often accompany end-stage alcoholism, for four years preceding the visions of 1799.

He was nursed in his illness by his married daughter, and he reportedly was able to do very little for himself. Some accounts suggest his bare-bones cabin was located quite close to the river, for he recalled hearing the drunken play—and fighting—of the raftsmen nearby. He thus had a long period of time in which he had little do but contemplate the effects of alcohol abuse, on his own life and on the lives of his tribesmen. In his code, he refers again and again to the "demons" afflicting the Seneca, and alcohol is clearly the primary demon he has in mind.

On the summer afternoon when Handsome Lake woke from his coma, he immediately began describing his vision to the family and friends who had gathered in preparation for his funeral.

Handsome Lake said:

> *Never have I seen such a wondrous vision. I saw three men clothed in fine raiment, noble and commanding, cheeks painted red, only a few feathers in their bonnets. They had in one hand bows and arrows, in the other, huckleberry bushes and berries of every color.*
>
> *The first messenger said:* "*He who created the world employed us to come to earth and go to the sick man and help him recover. Take these berries and eat of every color, for they will give you strength. Before noon, the people*

# The Code of Handsome Lake

*will gather at the council house and give you some early strawberries and they will make strawberry wine sweetened with sugar. They will drink the juice of the berry and thank the Great Spirit for your recovery.*

*"When you are well, we will tell you how things ought to be upon the earth. For whatsoever you think is evil, is evil."*

*And the second messenger said: "Behold! Look through the valley and between the two hills. Look between the sunrise and the noon. In that place, a man is buried who refused to obey the Great Spirit. He will never rise from that spot!*

*"So now we say to you, proclaim the message we give you and tell it truly to all the people."*

*And the third messenger said: "Now, the first thing has been finished and it remains for us to uncover all wickedness before you."*

*And the first messenger said: "Now it is time for our departure. We shall go on a journey. And then you will see the coming of the fourth messenger. And more: You will see the house of the punisher and the lands of the Great Spirit."*

\* \* \*

In addition to telling Handsome Lake that he would recover, and why they appeared, the messengers clearly promised that they would return with more messages from the Great Spirit. This seemed to have had an immediate effect on Handsome Lake: He would proclaim that he was cured of his alcoholism on this day. And his life seemed to change in another crucial respect: he had a new purpose in life, as a teacher and prophet. He began preaching what he called *Gaiwiio* (the good word), and his life from this day on would be dedicated to bringing the message of the Great Spirit (via the messengers) to the Seneca and taking an active role in improving the lives of his people.

The dream vision of this June day was only the first—if most dramatic—of a series of three or four visitations Handsome Lake would have over the next few years. He would also be visited by the spirits of John the Baptist, as well as a number of Jesus's disciples. The lessons Handsome Lake took from the visions would be compiled into The Code of Handsome Lake. The document (as taken down in translation) had some fifteen sections in the form of anecdotes that illustrated particular points.

One example:

> *Now the Great Spirit ordained that people should live to an old age: He appointed that when a woman becomes old she should be without strength and unable to work. Now the Great Spirit says that it is a great wrong to be unkind to our grandmothers. The Great Spirit forbids unkindness to the old. We, the messengers, say it. The Great Spirit appointed it this way: He designed it so that an old woman should be as a child again and when she becomes so, the Creator wishes the grandchildren to help her; for only because she is, they are. Whosoever does right to the aged does right in the sight of the Creator.*

For Handsome Lake, the first issue at hand was to condemn the use of the white man's *one'ga*, meaning whiskey. Since first contact, alcohol abuse had made serious inroads in the life of his nation, threatening its very extinction. As Arthur C. Parker described the situation:

> *The frauds which the Six Nations had suffered, the loss of land and of ancient seats had reduced them to poverty and disheartened them. The crushing blow of Sullivan's campaign was yet felt and the wounds then inflicted were fresh. The national order of the Confederacy was destroyed. Poverty, the sting of defeat, the loss of ancestral homes, the memory of broken promises, and the hostility of the white settlers all conspired to bring despair. There is not much energy in despairing nations who see themselves hopeless and alone, the greedy eyes of their conquerors fastened on the few acres that remain to them. It was little wonder that the Indian sought forgetfulness in the trader's rum.*

Many of the lessons in the Code address social or cultural problems and impart what might be called middle-class values: young people should marry, be kind and faithful to one another and be good to their children. They should not gossip, practice witchcraft or drink alcohol. In all, the sentiments expressed are strikingly similar to the biblical Ten Commandments. There is some evidence that Handsome Lake might have been familiar with the Bible: One story holds that his nephew Henry Obail (Abeal), who had been educated at a white institution in Philadelphia, took Handsome Lake up into the mountains and explained the Christian Bible to him. Handsome Lake might also have acquired some knowledge of the Bible from missionaries. At any rate, the Code, like the Bible, forbade drunkenness, witchcraft,

# The Code of Handsome Lake

sexual promiscuity, wife beating, quarreling and gambling.

But this is not to suggest that the Code wasn't revolutionary in its own way, for not only did it come from a Seneca, but Handsome Lake addressed the internal social ills that he believed were destroying Seneca culture just as surely as the intrusion of the white man. He took on taboo topics such as child sexual abuse, spousal abuse, adultery, divorce and abortion. Significantly, Handsome Lake addressed the men in his society in the same way that some modern groups like Promise Keepers and Concerned Black Men call on the males of their communities to be good husbands and fathers.

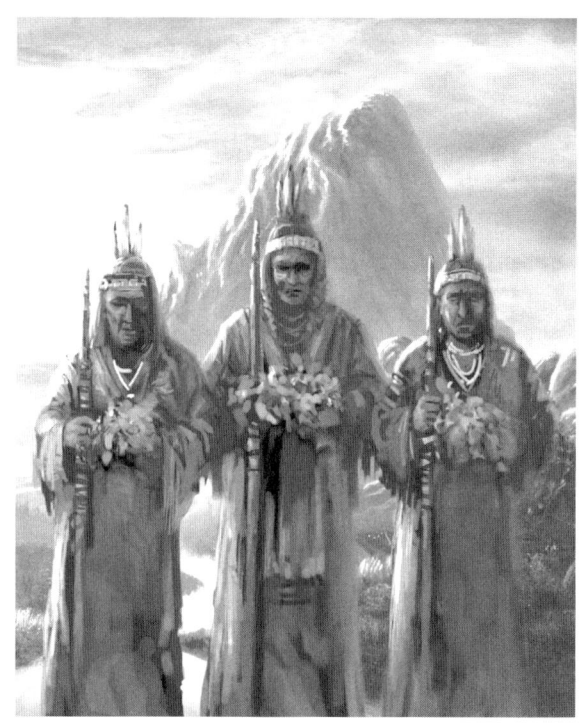

An illustration of the "Three Messengers" who were sent by the Great Ruler to teach Handsome Lake a new moral code.

Other parts of the Code dealt with the practicalities of life. In particular, Handsome Lake argued that the Seneca should give up the nomadic way of life and adopt an agricultural lifestyle. This is another example of his advocacy of what might be called middle-class values, even what would become the American dream of a farm, a home and a family. He advocated practical, orderly self-sufficiency and sober living.

It is clear that Handsome Lake was in critical ways a realist. He believed that the white man was here to stay, and that the Seneca could not survive and prosper by fighting the larger culture or falling into the trap of blaming the intruders for their conditions. This set him on a collision course with factions of his own community as well as for openly discussing these difficult issues within the Seneca Nation. This was a middle way, neither a capitulation to Christianity nor an unreasoning hold on the traditional past.

In fact, Handsome Lake's message was a masterful blend of the old and new. In order to appreciate the effect that Handsome Lake had on his people, it is perhaps necessary to point out that the Iroquois of the Great Lakes region had always considered dreams to be a guide to their lives. Their dreams influenced many decisions, from where to hunt or fish to where and when to make war or undertake marriage. Dreaming was believed to be a period in which the individual was in contact with the sacred power, and messages received during that time were taken with utmost seriousness. To ignore these messages was to court illness, madness or disaster. In fact, the Iroquois paid particular attention to dreams on the eve of big events, like war and hunting, and war parties were known to turn back if one of its members had an ominous dream.

For this reason, it may be fair to say that Handsome Lake's followers took his dreams, or visions, as seriously as he did. His dreams also represented answers to questions they were facing that were as momentous as war and hunting—that is, issues of the life and death of the nation.

In 1802, Handsome Lake visited Washington, D.C., with a delegation of Seneca and Onondaga chiefs, and his work drew the attention of U.S. president Thomas Jefferson, who wrote a letter to Handsome Lake that concluded:

> *Go on then, brother, in the great reformation you have undertaken. Persuade our red brethren then to be sober, and to cultivate their lands; and their women to spin and weave for their families. You will soon see your women and children well fed and clothed, your men living happily in peace and plenty, and your numbers increasing from year to year. It will be a great glory to you to have been the instrument of so happy a change, and your children's children, from generation to generation, will repeat your name with love and gratitude forever. In all your enterprises for the good of your people, you may count with confidence on the aid and protection of the United States, and on the sincerity and zeal with which I am myself animated in the furthering of this humane work. You are our brethren of the same land; we wish your prosperity as brethren should do. Farewell.*

This letter is a remarkable document, for it shows Thomas Jefferson's respect for the Indians and his willingness and hope of working with them to achieve peace and a good relationship. It also served as an endorsement of Handsome Lake's activities and program, and copies of it were given to each of the chiefs of the six nations.

# The Code of Handsome Lake

\* \* \*

Handsome Lake, like countless recovered addicts and social reformers, could sometimes be unreasoning and overzealous. This is particularly true when it came to the question of witchcraft among the Seneca.

By some accounts, Handsome Lake became obsessed with witch hunting and demanded confessions from those whom he suspected of witchcraft. There is evidence that some of those who refused to confess were killed on his orders. His obsession nearly started a war with another tribe when he accused one its members of being a witch, and he demanded that tribal leaders punish the young man. His obsessive hunting of witches began to cost him support among his people, and his popularity declined for a period.

According to one account, when he first arrived at Tonawanda, Handsome Lake was so discouraged that he was reluctant to talk about his visions and beliefs. Over time, however, people became friendlier, and he resumed his teachings. He was invited to visit the Onondaga, and he accepted the invitation, although "according to his visions it necessitated the singing of his 'third song,' which meant that he would die." But in another vision, the messengers said: "They have stretched out their hands, pleading for you to come and they are your own people at Onondaga."

So Handsome Lake and some followers started to walk to the Onondaga, and the numbers increased as they neared the destination, as people began to hear about his prediction of his own death. Handsome Lake had more visions along the way, each containing omens of his own death. He reportedly grew more and more depressed, even fearful. He was so distressed that, upon arrival, he was unable to address those who came to hear him, saying, "I will soon go to my new home. Soon will I step into the new world, for there is a plain pathway before me leading there."

He then went to his cabin, attended by three persons, who swore to keep all the details of his death secret. On August 10, 1815, Handsome Lake "commenced his walk" over the path that had appeared before him. He was buried under a nearby council house with impressive ceremonial rites. His tomb may still be seen there. It is marked by a granite monument erected by the Six Nations to Sedwa'gowa'ne: Our Great Teacher.

\* \* \*

Despite Handsome Lake's excesses and failings, he had a profound and lasting impact on the life of the Seneca and of the entire Iroquois nation. As the noted Indian scholar Arthur C. Parker wrote, "Handsome Lake helped to give the Iroquois a social and cultural identity that drew on the best of their traditional past, yet allowed them to turn their attention to finding a new way to live within the larger nation in which they now found themselves."

Handsome Lake's Code was so successful because it combined traditional Iroquois values and cultural forms with white and Christian values, allowing the Indians to adapt to their new circumstances. It emphasized practical strategies for survival without requiring the sacrifice of an Indian identity.

Handsome Lake's teachings long outlived him. Beginning in the 1820s, it became traditional for the Code to be recited every September at Tonawanda and biannually at other reservations in connection with the beginning of Six Nation meetings. The Code of Handsome Lake was eventually compiled and translated from interviews with descendants of Handsome Lake and published in 1913, ensuring that his teachings remain a part of Iroquois culture.

## CHAPTER 5
# The Psychic Highway

In 1800, the year after Handsome Lake had his first vision, Colonel Nathaniel Rochester arrived in the upstate New York area. It may be fair to say that Colonel Rochester had a vision of his own, though it was probably much more modest than what the town he founded would become.

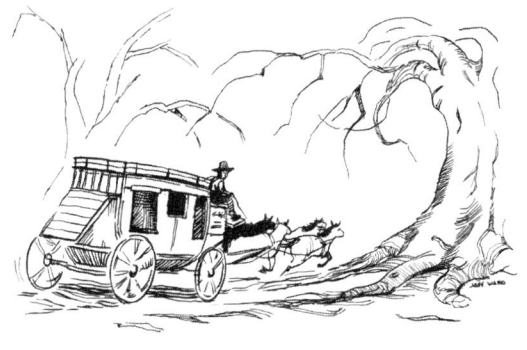

Colonel Rochester (1763–1831) was born in Virginia, but his family soon moved to North Carolina. By age twenty-one, he was a partner in a retail business and active in local and colonial politics. He served in the Revolutionary Army and then returned to Hillsborough, where he served as county clerk and colonel of the North Carolina militia. He eventually resigned most of these duties and entered into a business partnership with Thomas Hart, a wealthy merchant and land speculator. The two moved to Maryland in 1780 for greater business opportunities. There, Rochester married a local woman, Sophia Beatty, who would go on to bear him twelve children, one of whom, Thomas, would become the sixth mayor of the city of Rochester.

By the turn of the century, Colonel Rochester was once again looking for business opportunities. He and two business partners set out on horseback

# Folklore and Legends of Rochester

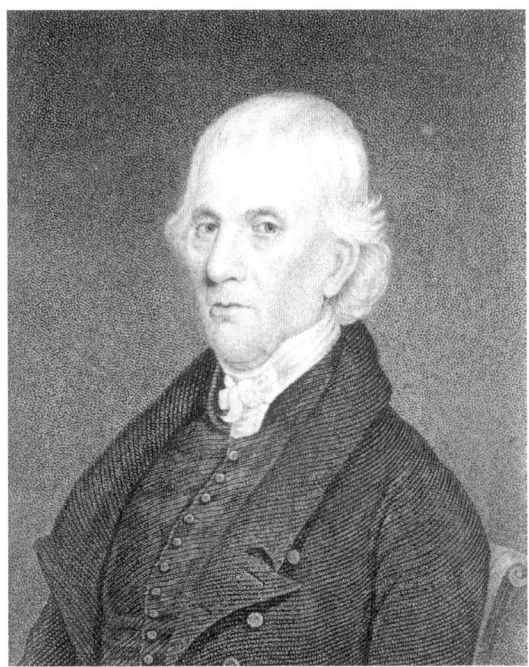

Nathaniel Rochester, 1752–1831, purchased one hundred acres of "swamp land" for $1,750. The parcel would later become the city of Rochester. *Courtesy of Rochester Public Library.*

on a prospecting trip to the frontier lands of New York. His partners acquired land along the upper portion of the Genesee River during their trip, but Rochester, sensing the opportunity to develop a town, chose instead a 120-acre tract along Canaseraga Creek, near Dansville. When the three men returned on a later trip, they traveled even farther up the river to a small abandoned tract of land—containing Indian Allan's mill—near the river's Upper Falls. The men saw a business opportunity, as any goods that traveled up the river would need to be unloaded here, and portage fees could be charged. They purchased 100 acres of land around the falls for $1,750.

In 1810, Rochester relocated his family to the area so that he could manage the land he now owned along the Genesee. The family established a homestead at Dansville.

Rochester quickly established numerous businesses and mills in the area and played an active role in the early politics of the town. He was so busy, in fact, that he didn't have time to devote to his Upper Falls land parcel, and Rochester offered to sell his interest to one of his business partners. The man declined. So, in 1811, Colonel Rochester—battling snakes, mosquitoes and malaria—began establishing a town on the Upper Falls tract. The first major road was cut through the woods: East Avenue, which was then four miles long, from Orringh Stone Tavern to the river. Rochester laid out other streets and established plots of land for municipal, church and business use. Later that year, he began to offer the plots for sale and named the would-be settlement Rochesterville. By 1812, there were new houses among the trees. Rochesterville would eventually become known as the "gateway to the West."

# The Psychic Highway

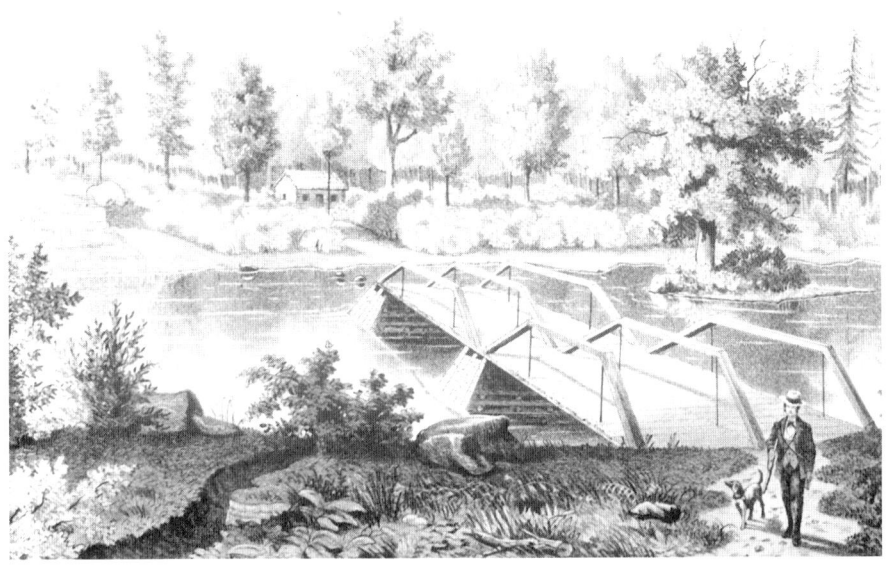

An illustration of Main Street Rochester, 1812. By 1860, Rochester was bigger than Chicago. *Courtesy of Rochester Public Library.*

## CLINTON'S DITCH

From the earliest days of the expansion of the English colonies from the eastern seaboard into the heartland of the continent, transportation was a problem. Close to the seacoast, rivers often provided adequate waterways, but the presence of the Allegheny Mountains a few hundred miles inland presented a great challenge. Passengers and freight had to travel overland, a journey made more difficult by the rough condition of the roads. Poor transportation hindered military operations and economic growth and led to political unrest as well, like the Whiskey Rebellion of the 1790s. The farther the expansion to the West, the clearer the problem became. The principal export product of the Ohio Valley was grain. And grain was a high-volume, low-priced commodity, often not worth the cost of transporting it to faraway population centers on the eastern coast.

Beginning in the late eighteenth century, many people began considering ways to solve the problem of linking the East Coast to the new western settlements. Cadwallader Colden first proposed using the Mohawk Valley in 1724. George Washington led a serious effort to turn the Potomac River into a navigable link to the west, sinking substantial capital into the Potowmack Canal from 1785 until his death. It was clear to many that the city or state that succeeded in developing a cheap, reliable route to the west would enjoy economic success. Thus, many proposals were created in Virginia, Maryland, Pennsylvania and New York.

Many New Yorkers believed that the key to development of the western part of the state was transportation. There were few existing roads, and many were poorly connected. Travel was long, expensive and difficult. The potential of the Mohawk Valley was clear: it runs east to west and cuts a natural pathway between the Catskills to the south and the Adirondacks to the north. The Mohawk River, a tributary of the Hudson, runs in a glacial meltwater channel across the Appalachians in the state, creating the valley. The Mohawk Valley was the only cut across the Appalachians north of Alabama, and it led almost directly from the Hudson River in the east to Lake Ontario and Lake Erie in the west. From there, much of the interior and many settlements would be accessible by the Great Lakes and rivers. The first proposal for a canal from Lake Ontario was made to the New York legislature in 1784. The proposal drew attention but little immediate action.

But the process had begun. New York governors Lewis Morris and Thomas Watson were other early proponents of a canal along the Mohawk. Their efforts led to creation of the Western Inland Lock Navigation Company, which took the first steps to improve navigation on the Mohawk, though the company could not take on such a project with only private financing. It was too big. Then, in 1798, the Niagara Canal Company was incorporated. The private individual who helped finally get the canal built was entrepreneur Jesse Hawley. He envisioned growing huge quantities of grain on the western New York plains—then largely unsettled—for sale on the eastern seaboard. He went bankrupt, however, trying to ship the grain to the coast. While in the Canandaigua debtors' prison, he started pressing for the construction of a canal from the eastern shore of Lake Erie to the upper Hudson River. He had strong support from Joseph Ellicott, an agent for the Holland Land Company in Batavia. Ellicott realized that a canal would add immense value to the land he was selling in the western part of the state. He would go on to become the first canal commissioner.

But the size and scale of the project was daunting. The land rises about six hundred feet from the Hudson to Lake Erie. Locks at the time could handle up to twelve feet, so at least fifty locks would be required along the 360-mile canal. It would have cost an unimaginable fortune. President Jefferson called the idea "a little short of madness" and rejected it. Nevertheless, Hawley managed to interest New York governor DeWitt Clinton in the idea.

# The Psychic Highway

Construction of the Erie Canal began July 4, 1817, at Rome, New York, and the final figures are mind boggling: the waterway, when finished, ran some 360 miles from Albany (on the Hudson River) to Buffalo (at Lake Erie), completing a navigable water route from the Atlantic Ocean to the Great Lakes. The channel was a cut 40 feet wide and 4 feet deep, with removed soil piled on the downhill side to form a walkway called the towpath. Canal boats, up to 3.5 feet in draft, would be pulled along the canal by horses and mules walking the towpath. The first 15 miles, from Rome to Utica, opened in 1819. At that rate, it would have taken thirty years for the canal to be finished.

There were numerous problems: felling trees to clear a path through virgin forest and moving excavated soil took much longer than expected initially, though the builders solved these problems. Other problems were that the sides of the cut were lined with stone set in clay, and the bottom was also lined with clay. The stonework required hundreds of masons. In fact, the supply of labor was one of the central problems of the project, and that included skilled, unskilled and professional manpower.

The young United States had no civil engineers, and much of the work was done by amateurs, though skilled ones at that. James Geddes and Benjamin Wright, who laid out the route, were judges whose experience in surveying was in settling boundary disputes. Geddes had only used a surveying instrument for a few hours when he took the job. Another key figure was Canvass White, a twenty-seven-year-old amateur engineer, who persuaded Governor Clinton to let him go to England at his own expense to study the canal system there. Nathan Roberts was a mathematics teacher and land speculator. Yet, as one historian put it, these men "carried the Erie Canal up the Niagara escarpment at Lockport, maneuvered it onto a towering embankment to cross over Irondequoit Creek, spanned the Genesee River on an awesome aqueduct, and carved a route for it out of the solid rock between Little Falls and Schenectady—and all of those venturesome designs worked precisely as planned."[9] It was an engineering marvel for its day. It included eighteen aqueducts to carry the canal over ravines and rivers and eighty-three locks.

The project changed the social makeup of the region, as it prompted a wave of immigration. Many of the laborers working on the canal were Scots-Irish who had recently come to the United States as a group of about five thousand from Northern Ireland, most of whom were Protestants and wealthy enough to pay for this caravan. Many of the masons who lined the cuts were German. Many French Canadians were drawn across the river to find work as unskilled laborers. When the canal reached Montezuma

Marsh (at the outlet of Cayuga Lake west of Syracuse), over one thousand laborers died of swamp fever. Construction came to a halt in that area, though it continued on the downhill slide toward the Hudson. Finally, when the marsh froze in winter, the crews returned to complete the section across the swamps.

Problems with the canal project roiled state politics in this period. During Governor Clinton's term, the New York State Constitutional Convention of 1821 shortened the gubernatorial term to two years and moved the beginning of the term from July 1 to January 1, effectively lopping off the last six months of the three-year term to which Clinton had been elected. Clinton then failed in his bid for renomination by his own party to run for reelection in November 1822, though he kept his post as president of the Erie Canal Commission. In April 1824, a majority of his political enemies, the Bucktails, voted in the New York legislature for his removal from the canal commission. This caused such a public outcry that he was nominated for governor by the People's Party and beat his own home party's candidate in the election. Clinton would be elected to another two terms as governor of New York and then die suddenly in office in 1828.

But he saw his project through to completion. When the Erie Canal officially opened on October 26, 1825, Governor Clinton marked the occasion by sailing in the packet boat *Seneca Chief*, among a flotilla, along the Erie Canal into Buffalo. After sailing from the mouth of Lake Erie to

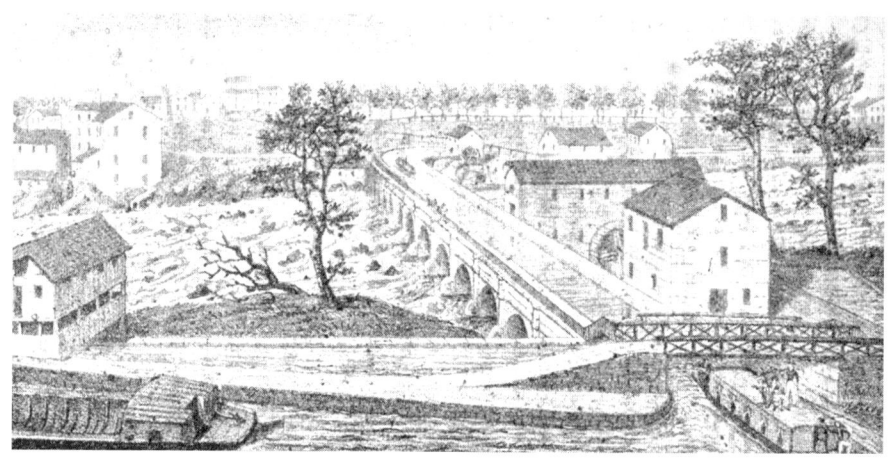

Construction of Erie Canal begins in 1817. The canal was a major catalyst for Rochester's growth. To accommodate population surge, the Farmers' Tavern and Inn was constructed. *Courtesy of Rochester Public Library.*

## The Psychic Highway

New York City, he emptied two casks of water from Lake Erie into New York Harbor, celebrating the first connection of waters from east to west. The event was marked statewide by a "Grand Celebration," culminating in successive cannon shots along the length of the canal and the Hudson River, a ninety-minute cannonade from Buffalo to New York City.

The Erie Canal entered American popular culture. Many writers took it as a subject, including Herman Melville, Nathaniel Hawthorne, Harriet Beecher Stowe and Mark Twain, among others. In 1824, before the canal was completed, a detailed *Pocket Guide for the Tourist and Traveler, Along the Line of the Canals, and the Interior Commerce of the State of New York* was published for the benefit of travelers and land speculators—possibly America's first tour guide. Some called it the Eighth Wonder of the World.

The canal was an enormous success, carrying vast numbers of passengers and huge amounts of freight. It was the first transportation system between the eastern seaboard and the western interior that did not require portage, was faster than carts pulled by draft animals and cut shipping costs by 90 percent. The canal fostered a population surge in western New York State, opened regions farther west to settlement and helped New York City become the chief U.S. port.[10]

The Erie Canal was a crucial catalyst for the development of Rochester. The journey from Albany to Buffalo was shortened dramatically, from two weeks overland to a few days by water. Shipbuilding would eventually become Rochester's second largest industry. The quickly growing city, then on the edge of the American frontier, became known as the "Young Lion of the West." Ebenezer Allen's mill turned out to be only the first of many mills in the city. By 1838, flour milling was the city's largest industry, and Rochester produced more flour than any other American city, giving it another moniker: "Flour City."

*\*\*\**

One of the men drawn to Rochester by all the activity taking place in the area was Erastus Granger (1765–1825). Originally from Suffield, Connecticut, Granger arrived in the state of New York in 1804, carrying papers from President Thomas Jefferson that authorized him to become the first postmaster general in western New York. He moved to a small settlement then known as New Amsterdam, which would eventually become Buffalo (a city that also shared an original name with New York City). Granger was also collector of the port. In 1807, he was appointed as a judge in Genesee County, and soon thereafter, he moved to Rochesterville. He would also, by the way, go on to become a key figure in negotiations between the U.S. government and the Iroquois Confederacy, in the process of which he developed a complicated relationship with Chief Red Jacket, the arch rival of Handsome Lake.

Granger found himself in a city undergoing rapid growth, and he sought to take advantage of it. Building an inn was a logical business decision, as the city now served as an important transit point for travelers heading toward the western frontier. He built the first known structure on what would later become known as Hoodoo Corner, the Farmers' Tavern and Inn. In 1823, he organized a "raising bee," and along with twelve local men, he built the structure situated on the corner of Main and Elm Streets. He both owned and managed the inn until his death in 1826. The Farmers' Tavern and Inn would stand until 1893, when it was finally torn down to make way for Carroll's Department Store, which eventually became McCurdy's.

Within a few years of its establishment, the Farmers' Tavern and Inn became well known for its "noisy" ghost. The origin of this ghost is not clear: there are no known murders that occurred on the site—at least in the hotel itself—although there were reportedly a number of suicides. It was said that a ghost inhabited a particular room on the second floor of the inn. Hotel staff reportedly rented the room only when every other room was occupied. There were numerous accounts of the unlucky folks who ended up in the room being roused from their sleep in the middle of the night, flying out of the room and making their way quickly downstairs to complain about the commotion.

It should be noted that this establishment was both a tavern and an inn. A tavern, in those days, was similar to a British pub. It was a neighborhood spot, a place for locals to gather for a drink, to discuss the news, to gossip and to socialize. The primary function of an inn was, as the name suggests, to provide lodging for travelers, both business and pleasure. But in the eighteenth century, another primary function of an inn was to provide longer-term housing and meals for workingmen of various sorts. They were often young and single, moving around in accordance with working seasons or the dictates of their own wanderlust. Thus the Farmers' Tavern and Inn attracted a diverse crowd of both the socially prominent and those on the edges of society. And the conditions a traveler found at a tavern or inn were highly variable.

One newspaper of the time published a slightly tongue-in-cheek account of one such experience:

> *A weary and hungry traveler on a jaded horse rode up to the door of one [tavern]...and asked for entertainment for the night. The landlady from within having assented, the following colloquy ensued:*
> *Traveler: "Can you furnish provender for my horse?"*
> *Landlady: "No, we have none."*
> *Traveler: "Can you furnish me with supper?"*
> *Landlady: "We have no bread. My husband started for the mill this morning and will return tomorrow."*
> *Traveler: "Can you furnish me with a glass of whiskey?"*
> *Landlady: "We have none. My husband took his gallon bottle, and will bring some when he returns."*
> *Traveler: "Madam, can you tell me what you do keep for the entertainment of travelers?"*
> *Landlady: "We keep a tavern, sir."*[11]

Contemporary descriptions of some of the establishments in the area paint a vivid picture of the atmosphere that often prevailed. Of nearby Gansen's Inn, one man wrote: "It is a miserable log house. We made out to obtain an ordinary dinner. Our landlord was drunk; the house was crowded with a dozen workmen, reeking with rain and sweat. We hastened our departure before the rain had ceased."[12]

A place like Farmers' Tavern and Inn, in other words, was a gathering spot for all kinds of people who might not ordinarily come into contact with one another. And this was particularly true of Rochester in this period. It is hard to overstate the phenomenal growth the city was undergoing: by 1829, only fifteen years after its founding, Rochester's population was already eight thousand. Almost by definition, the first inhabitants of any newly settled place were risk takers, people who were on the move, perhaps dissatisfied with life in the more settled areas of the country and thus in search of something new. They were people who were not averse to living without the comforts of life in settled areas and were, in fact, mostly laboring men—the sort who would be laying the physical foundation for those who would follow them. This trend was well underway in Rochester by the late 1820s and would virtually explode in the next decade.

All of this gives us another possible clue to the reason this spot became known as Hoodoo Corner, in the sense of the term meaning "jinx."

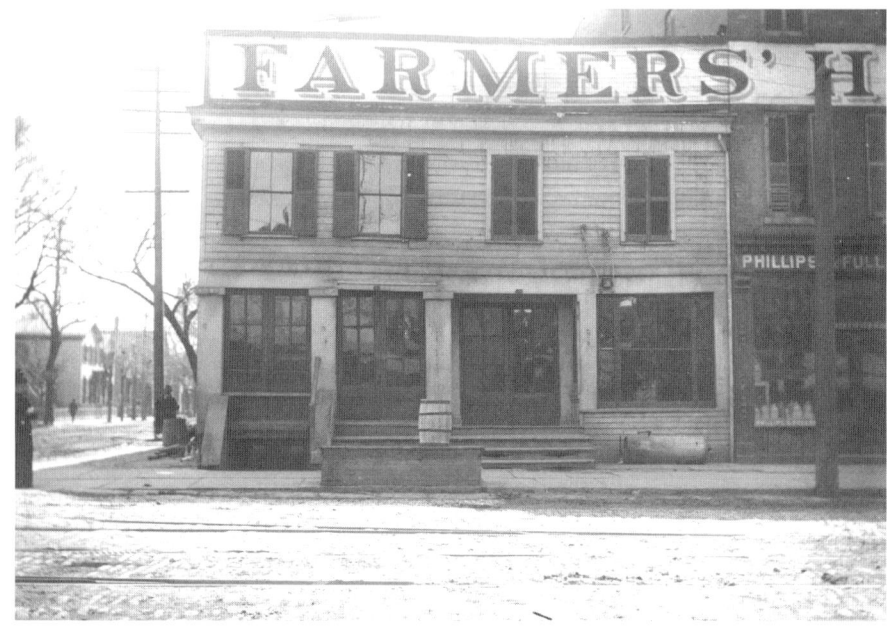

Farmers' Tavern and Inn, located at Main and Elm Streets. Some believed that Octavius Barron hid there after murdering William Lyman. *Courtesy of Rochester Museum & Science Center.*

Farmers' Tavern and Inn was certainly the site of drunken bar fights; the place that drew men who were moving, or on the run, from one thing or another; and the kind of men who were not averse to drinking, gambling, discussing politics and arguing about all of it. As we shall see in the stories of Captain William Morgan and William Lyman, it was a highly combustible environment.

The Farmers' Tavern and Inn was the kind of place that one might be a little nervous going into, a place where the atmosphere might change suddenly, becoming more tense and dangerous. In that frame of mind, it's not hard to see how the idea of a jinx, or a curse, could become attached to a place over time, alive as it was as well with legends of an Indian burial ground and hoodoo structures nearby.

## CHAPTER 6
# The Strange Disappearance of Captain William Morgan

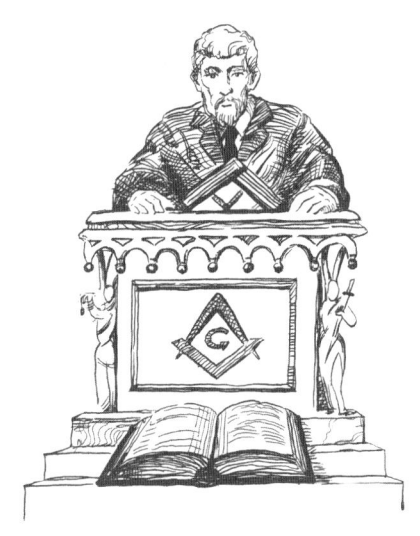

"Murder! Murder!" cried the man, as he struggled with the two men who, having just bailed him out of Canandaigua Jail, took him by both arms as he stepped out the door. The cries brought Mary Hall to her window, where she watched the scuffle in front of the jail. She recognized the two men, Lawson and Foster, who had accosted the third and later named them for the authorities. And Hall noticed a group of men, perhaps three or four, standing near the end of the street, and yet another pair of men standing a short distance away, perhaps a half block. But none of these men moved to offer any assistance to the struggling man.

Then one of the men not far from the jail, who seemed to be watching the progress of the struggle with interest (she would later identify him as Colonel Edward Sawyer), took his cane and rapped hard on the curb with it, an apparent signal to the carriage waiting just down the street. The carriage driver ordered his two gray horses forward—passing directly in front of Hall's house, though she couldn't make out who the driver was—and drew up next to the group of struggling men.

While continuing to "cry in the most distressing manner," the man struggled with all his might against the other two, until "his voice appeared to be suppressed by something put over his mouth." Lawson and Foster forcibly loaded the man into the carriage, and it drove off down the street. Hall continued to watch. When the carriage had disappeared, Colonel Sawyer leaned over and picked up the hat that was left lying in the street. It had been knocked from the head of the kidnapped man during the struggle.

It was nearly 9:00 p.m. on September 12, 1826. The men that Hall and others identified as being outside the jail that night were all Freemasons. And Captain William Morgan, the struggling man who cried out, would never be seen again.

\*\*\*

A contemporary visitor to Batavia, New York, might come across a monument there to Captain William Morgan, erected in 1882 by the National Christian Association, a group opposed to secret societies. The inscription on the monument reads: "Sacred to the memory of William Morgan, a native of Virginia, a Captain in the War of 1812, a respectable citizen of Batavia, and a martyr to the freedom of writing, printing, and speaking the truth. He was abducted from near this spot in the year 1826, by Freemasons, and murdered for revealing the secrets of their order."

The apparent historical tidiness of this inscription, however, may be misleading. Almost two hundred years later, it is clear that Morgan was abducted in 1826, and it is generally acknowledged that the kidnapping was the work of Freemasons. But the reason(s) for the abduction—and perhaps most importantly, the eventual fate of the man himself—is still a matter of research and speculation. It remains one of American history's great mysteries.

The facts of Morgan's early life are hazy, but he is believed to have been born in Culpeper County, Virginia, in 1774. He moved around frequently, including periods in Rochester, Canada and Richmond, Virginia. In 1819, the forty-four-year-old Morgan married sixteen-year-old Lucinda Pendleton, who would eventually give him two children. Morgan claimed that his rank as a captain came from his service in the War of 1812, though there is some doubt to this assertion. He also apparently worked a variety of jobs, including stints as a brewer, bricklayer and stonecutter before he finally

## The Strange Disappearance of Captain William Morgan

settled in Batavia in the early 1820s, where he quickly acquired a reputation as a drinker and gambler.

His kidnapping was precipitated by a series of events that began in early 1826, when a petition was initiated to start a Masonic chapter in Batavia. Morgan was eligible for membership in this chapter by virtue of his professional qualifications and perhaps because he had been a member of another chapter. But Morgan's name was not on the petition. When he found out, Morgan petitioned for approval to add his name as a founding member of the new chapter, which was granted. But there were apparently some Freemasons who objected to Morgan's inclusion—perhaps because of his reputation as a drunkard, perhaps because it was proved that he had lied on his application, claiming membership in another lodge, which he did not actually have. In any case, while Morgan was reportedly off on a drunken binge, the amended petition was destroyed; by whom has never been shown.

Yet another petition was started and again circulated without Morgan's name on it. When Morgan found out this had happened again, he became enraged. Besides the sting of rejection, the decision to exclude him could have profound consequences for Morgan's economic situation. Being denied membership would effectively deny him access to masonry jobs in the area. Morgan's anger turned to a desire for revenge, and he began talking quite publicly about his intention to publish a book that would reveal the inner secrets of the Masonic order.

To this end, Morgan joined forces with another local resident, David C. Miller. Miller had been rejected for membership by the Freemasons some years earlier. He was well known as the publisher of an anti-Masonic paper, and he reportedly offered Morgan a sizeable advance for the work. Morgan quickly completed the manuscript, and the book was registered with the clerk of the Northern District Court and accepted by the publisher in August 1826 under the title *Illustrations of Masonry by One of the Fraternity*.

Despite Morgan's disappearance, the book was eventually printed and still exists.[13] It was reportedly read by Joseph Smith, who incorporated elements of Masonic ritual into his new Church of Jesus Christ of Latter-day Saints. But Morgan's work is more than a catalog of practices—it is also an indictment of Freemasonry. In addition to describing the rituals and ceremonies of the Masonic order, including key signs, symbols and words, which were never to be revealed to any outsider by a brother, Morgan paints a disturbing picture of a power-hungry organization. He suggests that the Masonic Order might once have been a benevolent institution, but that it is now "naked and worthless." He wrote: "It works unseen, at all silent hours,

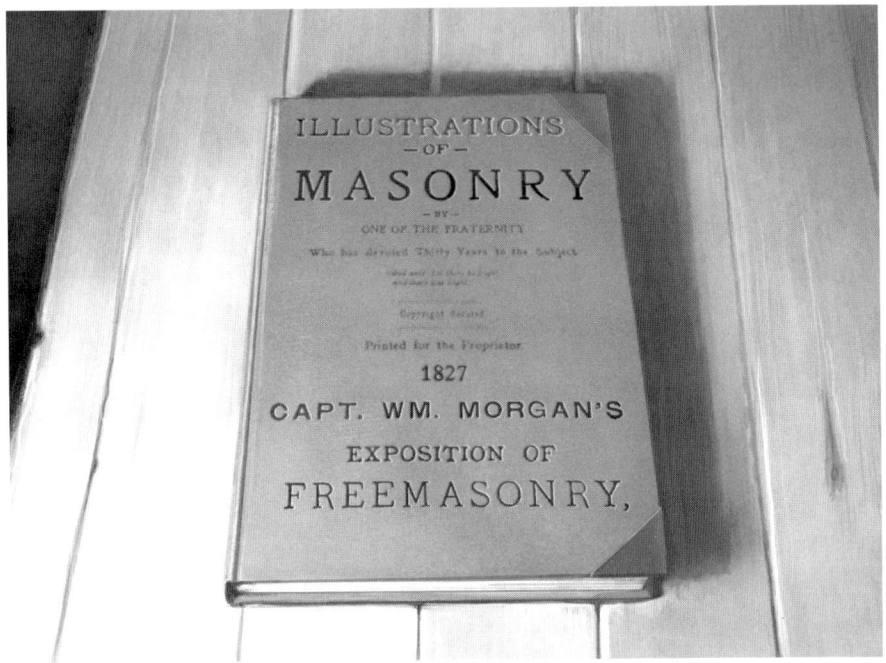

An illustration of William Morgan's book. Morgan's disappearance sparked an anti-Masonic movement and led to the first political third party in the United States.

and secret times and places; and, like death when summoning his diseases, pounces upon its devoted subject, and lays him prostrate in the dust. Like the great enemy of man, it has shown its cloven foot, and put the public upon its guard against its secret machinations." Most significantly, Morgan suggests, the secret nature of the "fraternity within a fraternity," in fact jeopardized the free functioning of legitimate civil and legal institutions in the then young United States.

At this point, something of an open war broke out between the Masons on one side and Morgan and Miller on the other. There were ads placed in a newspaper, warning Masons to avoid Morgan.[14] There were a number of attempts to prevent publication. Miller's offices, which contained his printing press, were set on fire more than once. Morgan was repeatedly harassed, including being arrested a number of times by sheriffs who were also Freemasons. Some of the charges appeared to be legitimate; others were apparently trumped up. In each case, Miller came to the rescue, bailing Morgan out of jail—until the night of September 12, 1826, that is, when the Freemasons altered their tactics.

# The Strange Disappearance of Captain William Morgan

On this evening, Morgan was walking down Main Street when he was arrested on a debt warrant and taken to the Canandaigua Jail. The charge was dismissed, and Morgan was then immediately rearrested on a charge of theft, for failing to return a shirt and tie he had borrowed. As Morgan sat in the jail cell, two men, claiming to be friends of his, came to post his bail. The men paid the $2.69 fine and demanded that Morgan be released. It just so happened that the jailer was away at the time, so the men convinced the jailer's wife to release Morgan into their custody. She did so, and the three men left the jail.

When Morgan stepped out the doors of the jail that evening, he was abducted, and never seen again. The account of the abduction is taken from the testimony of a number of witnesses in the vicinity of the jail that evening. The witness accounts are substantially the same, with the exception of the exact number of men who took part in the abduction. Out of six witnesses, all agree that two men exited the jail with Morgan, while others mention one, two or three groups of two men, or possibly three or four men, stationed at various points along the street, all of whom seemed to respond to the sight of Morgan as he stepped into the street. It is likely that some were innocent bystanders, while others were present to assist in the abduction.

## WHERE IS WILLIAM MORGAN?

The reaction to Morgan's disappearance was an overwhelming public uproar. It was immediately and widely suspected that the Masons were responsible for the crime, and this general belief was supported by the publication of a story in the *Telegraph*, a local Rochester paper.

The story was written by Thurlow Weed, the publisher of the paper. From the publication of this first article detailing the circumstances of Morgan's disappearance until his death in 1882, Weed was an integral part of the story of Captain Morgan. It seems fair to say that the abduction changed the course of Weed's life, as he became first the primary local opponent of the Freemasons due to the Morgan affair and then a national antagonist. Weed helped found the Anti-Masonic Party, the first political third party in American history, in 1828. And even on his deathbed, as we shall see, Weed had something to say about the Morgan affair.

Thurlow Weed (1797–1882) is a fascinating character in his own right. Born into a farming family in Cairo, New York, he received little formal education. By the age of eight, he was working on boats on the Hudson

River. He eventually became apprenticed to a printer and served as a very young man in the War of 1812. Afterward, he went to work running the presses for the *Albany Register* and soon began writing for the paper as well. He was apparently drawn to journalism, at least partly by political motives, as he immediately used this platform to support DeWitt Clinton and the Erie Canal policy.

In 1824, Weed supported the presidential bid of John Quincy Adams and helped ensure Adams's victory in New York. Weed also sought and won election that year to the New York State Assembly. There he met William H. Seward and began a lifelong personal and political friendship. In 1824, Weed took a job at the *Rochester Telegraph*, which he purchased in 1825.

It is probably fair to say that Weed's anti-Masonry feelings predated the Morgan affair and was part of a broader movement then coalescing in upstate New York. Much of the opposition to Freemasonry was along class lines. Many members of the political and social elite—judges, sheriffs, lawyers, businessmen, bankers and politicians—were Freemasons, and ordinary citizens began to view them as a closed group, whose primary loyalty lay with their own members rather than with notions of fairness or

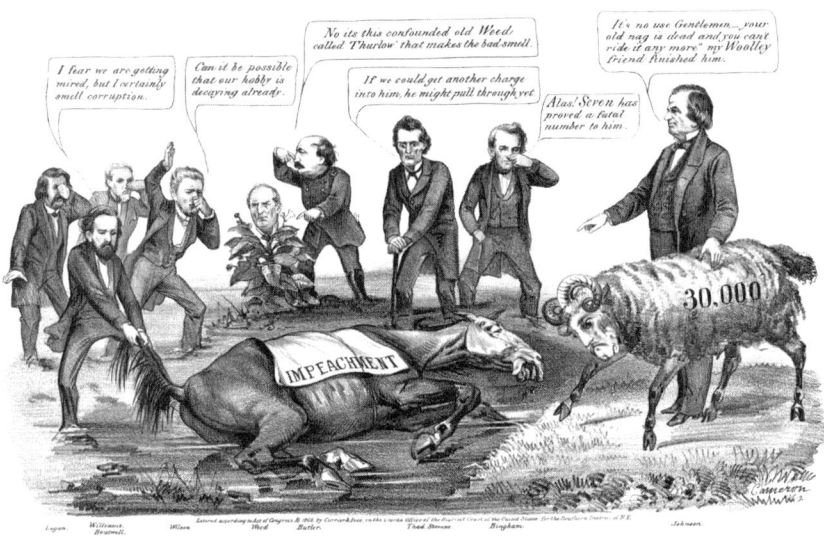

A lithograph depicting the failed impeachment of Andrew Johnson and role of Thurlow Weed. Weed rose to political prominence as a result of the Morgan affair. *Courtesy of Rochester Public Library.*

the rule of law. There was growing fear that the lodges' secret oaths bound the brethren to favor each other against outsiders in the courts as well as in other areas of life.

And if the disappearance of Captain Morgan crystallized anti-Mason sentiment among the general public, it seems to have radicalized Weed. In his memoir, Weed recounts his astonishment that his "six-line paragraph" on the Morgan kidnapping brought "dozens of our most influential citizens, greatly excited, to the office, stopping the paper, and ordering the discontinuance of their advertisements." Whether the individuals were Freemasons or perhaps businessmen who simply feared that being associated with an anti-Masonic paper might negatively affect their concerns, Weed does not say. In any case, Weed, either genuinely ignorant or feigning ignorance, then approached his business partner, Robert Martin, and asked what the *Telegraph* had done to "exasperate" so many people. According to Weed, Martin brought out a book and directed him to read a paragraph "invoking severe penalties for disclosing the secrets of the Masons."

Weed then resigned his position and elected to disassociate himself from the newspaper, for fear that it would be ruined by his continued presence. He attempted to find a job as an editor at two nearby newspapers but was refused in both cases, on the grounds that he "had been too busy in getting up an excitement about Morgan." Weed's outrage grew. At any rate, whether by default or by design, Weed now found himself with plenty of time to get more deeply involved in the Morgan affair.

The excitement surrounding the Morgan abduction continued with another dramatic incident occurring a few days later. According to an article entitled "Outrages Followed in Quick Succession" by Charles W. Miller (the son of David C. Miller, the publisher of Morgan's book on the Freemasons), two buildings belonging to the elder Miller, which housed a printing press and other equipment, were again set on fire, though it was doused. The next day, "a mob, consisting of more than a hundred, assembled in this village, from various parts of the country, with the openly avowed intention of destroying our printing establishment; and conveyed the Editor of this paper out of town by a ruffian force, pretending to have legal process." But the editor, David Miller, found when he reached the court at Le Roy that that there was no complaint on file nor did anyone appear to press a claim, and he was released. Charles Miller offers his testimony on behalf of his father who, he claims, "has ill health, brought on by continual excitement, [which] prevents him from giving in this number, a full development of these rascally outrages."[15]

## Is Morgan Found?

Nearly a month after Morgan's disappearance, it seemed that an answer to his whereabouts might be at hand when a body washed up on the shores of Lake Ontario. The man had evidently drowned. The coroner held an inquest and declared the body to be Morgan's. He claimed that a scar on one foot, and most significantly, a double row of teeth, matched the description that Lucinda Morgan had given of her husband. She did fail, however, to accurately describe or recognize the description of the clothing on the body and thus would not proclaim it publicly as that of her husband.

Thurlow Weed and others, possibly hoping to resolve the discrepancy or for a little more publicity, organized a second inquest a few days later. In what must have been a macabre scene, the corpse was disinterred from its resting place near the river's shore in the presence of some forty or fifty witnesses, including the coroner, and Lucinda Morgan was brought forward to positively identify the body. This time, she firmly pronounced it the body of her missing husband. Most people thought the matter was then settled.

A few weeks later, however, the coroner reversed his findings. He corrected his identification, saying that the body was not Morgan's after all, but rather that of Timothy Monroe, who had been proclaimed missing and presumed drowned some weeks before. But this identification was also problematic, because Monroe's widow had described her husband as being three to four inches shorter than the corpse, and she also described him as having hair that was "black and cut close to his head," while the corpse's hair was "long, silky, and of a chestnut color." But Mrs. Monroe, like Mrs. Morgan, had described her husband as having a double row of teeth, which matched the corpse. Significantly, Mrs. Monroe's description of the clothing was an exact match.

Therefore a third inquest was held, at which considerable time was given over to testimony about the socks that the corpse was wearing. Mrs. Monroe accurately described a darned patch on one of the toes, and finally, the body was declared to be that of Timothy Monroe.

As it turned out, however, the final outcome of the inquest is perhaps less important for its final determination of the identity of the deceased than its role in shaping the form that the public narrative of the case would take over the coming years. For, on the evening of the third inquest, Weed went to a local hotel to meet with a friend. When he was leaving, he happened to cross paths with Ebenezer Griffin, a local lawyer employed by the Masons. Griffin reportedly greeted Weed with the words: "Well, Weed, what will you do for a Morgan now?" To which, according to Weed, he replied: "That is a good enough Morgan for us till you bring back the one you carried off."

But the next morning, the *Daily Advertiser*, a Masonic paper, reported Weed as having answered: "That is a good enough Morgan for us until after the election." The alleged comment became a sensation, picked up by many newspapers and was repeated again and again by political partisans in the years to come.[16]

The reported comment undoubtedly gained such traction because it suggested a certain political opportunism at work on the part of the anti-Masons. But it also suggested, to some, another possible answer to the question of Morgan's whereabouts. If Weed and the anti-Masons were so willing to make political use of the Morgan affair, might they have an interest in seeing that Morgan didn't return? Or might they have played a role in creating the affair itself?

## Cui Bono?

It is commonplace in police investigations, when considering possible motives for a crime such as murder, to ask the question *cui bono?* It is Latin, meaning, who benefits? Who has the most to gain from the crime? One of the most interesting aspects of the Morgan affair is the fact that this question has many possible answers.

Although there were—and still are—some Freemasons who never accepted that members of their order were responsible for the abduction and presumed murder of William Morgan, by and large the organization (especially once passions cooled) tacitly accepted culpability for the crime. The most widely accepted theory as to the fate of Morgan—accepted by many Masons and non-Masons and apparently supported by some evidence and rumor—was that Morgan was driven directly on the night of his kidnapping to Fort Niagara, where he was delivered into the custody of a group of Masons and was eventually drowned in the Niagara River or Lake Ontario.

In this scenario, the logic of the crime is clear: the Masons killed Morgan both for revenge and to keep him quiet. He had betrayed the secrets of their order, and they intended to destroy the manuscript he had written, along with any copies that might have already been printed. This scenario also explains the attack on Miller's office.

But the fact that the Masons paid such a high price for the abduction of Morgan, and that publication of the manuscript went forward, has made

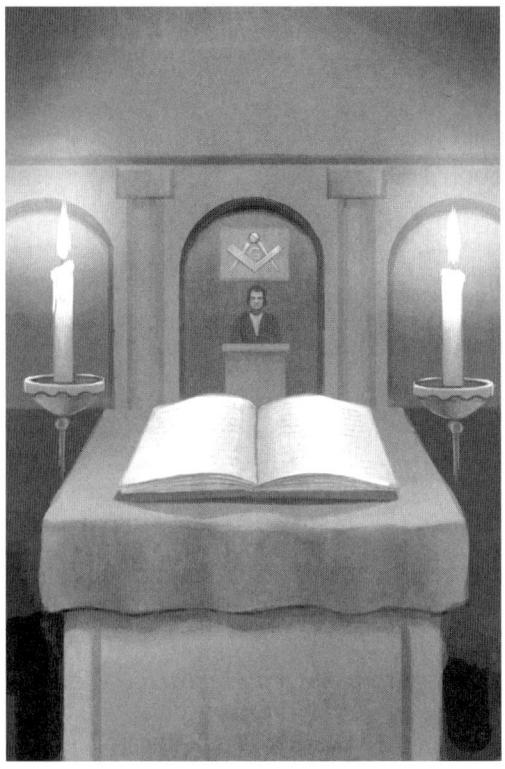

An illustration of a Masonic altar as seen in the documentary *The Strange Disappearance of Captain William Morgan*.

some question whether it makes sense at all to presume that they committed the crime. From the moment he disappeared, Morgan became a larger thorn in the side of the Masons than he was perhaps in his everyday life. Not only did the Morgan affair provide the anti-Masonic movement with a cause célèbre and an energetic and formidable leader in Weed, but it meant that the Masons were entangled in ongoing legal difficulties for years with concomitant bad publicity.

Over the course of many years, some fifty-seven people were arrested for the kidnapping, and at least eight grand jury proceedings took place. All told, twenty-eight individuals were brought to trial on charges having to do with the Morgan affair. Eventually, three Masons—Loton Lawson, Nicholas Chesebro and Edward Sawyer—were convicted of the kidnapping of Morgan. This meant that the facts of Morgan's abduction and the criminal proceedings stayed in the newspapers—and on the minds of the public—for years after the event.

Along the way, there were the predictable accusations of judicial misconduct as well as the more mundane errors that accompany many lengthy investigations and prosecutions, and the Masons, at the time, did everything in their power to resist further inquiries. The result was the inverse of what the Masons were hoping for. In fact, because the vast majority of the alleged conspirators went free, many New Yorkers concluded that Masons were constantly working behind the scenes, using their connections to official authority to protect themselves and promote the goal of the fraternity rather than to pursue justice. Many came to the conclusion that "if good government

## The Strange Disappearance of Captain William Morgan

was to be restored all Masons must be purged from public office," further fueling anti-Masonic sentiment.[17] In the following years, the Anti-Masonic Party elected forty congressmen and two state governors. And in 1832, they put forth a presidential candidate who won a quarter-million votes.

There has been speculation that perhaps the Masons were unfairly blamed for the entire affair. While there is little doubt that Masons initially kidnapped Morgan, there are competing theories about what happened afterward. As defenders of the Masons ask, what did they have to gain by killing him? His book had already gone to press, and the chances of finding and destroying every last copy of the manuscript or printed pages were slim. And Morgan, with his reputation as a drunkard and gambler, was not the most formidable of opponents. This contention is supported by evidence that Morgan plagiarized portions of his book. Moreover, rumors about the plagiarism had begun even before Morgan disappeared. Given this—and knowing that the disappearance of a vocal anti-Mason wouldn't go unnoticed—would the Masons have killed Morgan? And if they didn't, then what happened to him?

One theory, again supported by some evidence and rumor, was that Morgan was indeed kidnapped by the Freemasons and taken to Fort Niagara, where there was a convention of Canadian and American Masons. Morgan, in this scenario, was questioned and then offered a choice: he could settle on a farm in Canada with his family, or he could take $500 and a horse in return for his permanently leaving the area. There is some speculation that he chose the second option and was assured that the Masons would care for his family until they could be reunited, although such a reunification never came to pass.

In this theory, Morgan then went to Boston, a supposition that is based on a number of supposed sightings of him there the following year. A variation is that Morgan was given the horse and eventually passage aboard a ship. He then sailed, in one version, to Smyrna (located in present-day Turkey), based on a supposed sighting of him there by an American ship's captain in 1830. In another version of the story, Morgan sailed to Honduras or the Cayman Islands, where he lived to an old age.[18]

There is some evidence to suggest that Morgan's business partners in the book venture—Miller and a couple of investors, John David and Russell Dyer—were in fact souring on their partnership with Morgan, especially as evidence mounted that Morgan's book was not original but was largely stolen from an earlier work, published in France. In this scenario, Morgan, under threat from Miller and the others, began to fear for his life and, in fact, went to the Masons of Batavia and asked for their help. The abduction was then staged, allowing Morgan to escape the harassment he'd been suffering at the hands of the Masons as well as his responsibilities to his business partners and to his wife and children. Alternately, it is supposed that Miller and the other investors had some interest in having Morgan disappear, or at least stay disappeared, once he had. The logic is that Morgan's drinking and his tendency to hold court in local taverns might have led him to reveal that he'd indeed plagiarized his book, which would have negative consequences for sales and thus might have motivated the men to make sure Morgan didn't return to the area.

Yet another theory about the fate of Morgan rests on the fact that he was a well-known drunkard. In this scenario, it is supposed that the Masons might have abducted Morgan but not with the intention of killing him. He might, during his captivity, have suffered a fatal attack of the delirium tremens, commonly known as the DTs. Therefore, Morgan might have died within days of being abducted, but the cause might have been natural. In this scenario, the Masons intended to persuade him to alter his publication plans and keep him confined until this could be accomplished. This theory comes into play in connection with two particular locations, both of which, it has been claimed, are haunted by the ghost of Morgan.

## The Ghost of Morgan?

One interesting aspect of the two ghost stories is each contains a plausible explanation for how Morgan might have ended up in that location shortly after his abduction, depending on the route taken by the kidnappers. Assuming that Morgan's final destination was indeed Fort Niagara, there are two reasonable routes by which he might have been taken: the western route or the northern route.

The northern route would have taken Morgan past Hoodoo Corner, the corner of Main and Elm. This would have been a longer trip, though these roads were also far less traveled than the western route, which might have appealed to the men who were engaged in the abduction. Another rationale for going this way was that the Farmers' Tavern and Inn was one of the few places in the area that kept livery stables, which would have provided the kidnappers an opportunity to acquire fresh horses and perhaps alcohol for Morgan as well. They might have been concerned about the potential complications of transporting an alcoholic, who might quickly become ill if he went without alcohol for too long.

# The Strange Disappearance of Captain William Morgan

The western route, on the other hand, would have been more direct, but it had the disadvantage of being well traveled. A main stagecoach route, it would have taken Morgan by the American Hotel, in Lima, a location that he is believed to have frequented during his life. There were long-standing rumors that Morgan spent at least one night after the abduction in the area, perhaps at the hotel. Others maintained that he spent a much longer period in the area and, in fact, died there.

Speculation about the latter scenario increased after an odd incident in 1848. During a meeting of Freemasons at the American Hotel, someone stole the coats of the men who were inside. Then, a couple of weeks after the coats were stolen, they were returned—left outside the door of the hotel, neatly stacked and tied together—with a note of apology on top. It was soon determined that the coats had been intentionally infected with the smallpox virus. The act was clearly anti-Masonic in origin and may have been motivated by the belief that Morgan had died in the area.

The source of a long-standing rumor that Morgan lived in the Lima area after his abduction was finally identified by a book kept in a locked safe at

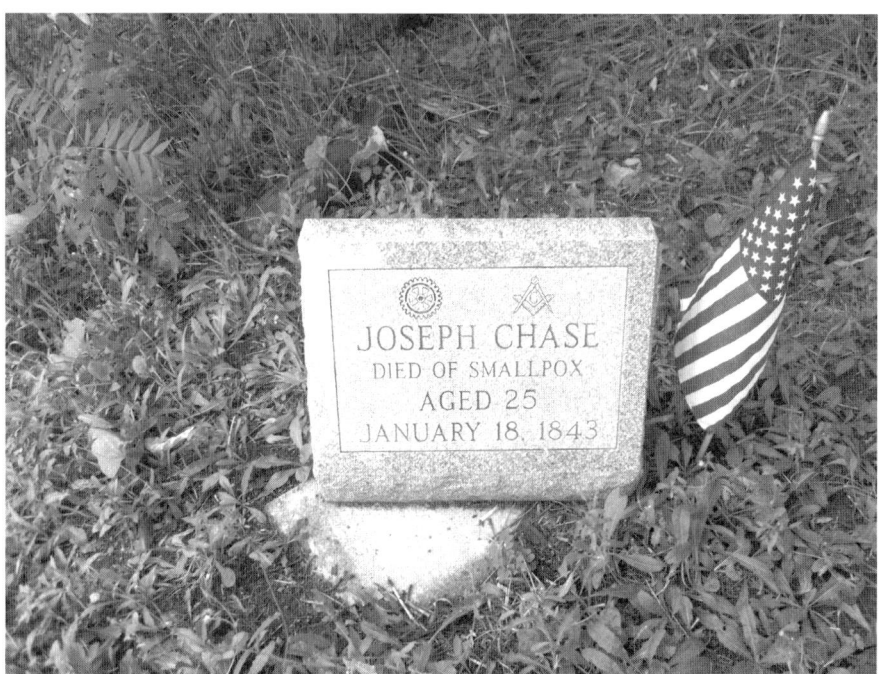

Grave site of a Mason believed to have died from smallpox after becoming infected while attending a lodge meeting at the American Hotel. *Courtesy of the author.*

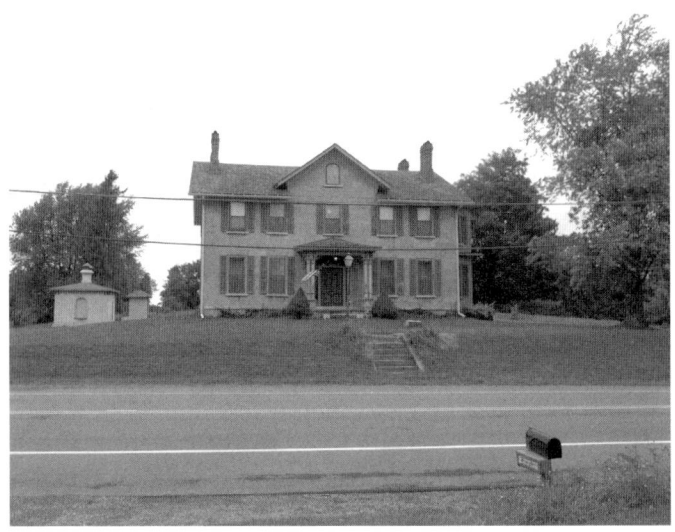

A current photograph of the house in Lima thought to have harbored William Morgan. It is believed by some that he haunts the house to this day. *Courtesy of the author.*

the Masonic Lodge in Batavia. While doing research for the documentary series that grew out of this research, I approached the Masons of Batavia for information, expecting that little would be forthcoming. But on a visit, the grandmaster of the lodge was quite friendly and forthcoming and led me down one hallway after another, until I found myself in a room with a huge safe. The man opened it, then a locked compartment within it and finally withdrew a little book, which had its own little lock as well.

The book, while confirming much of what I had read before, revealed that about a year after Morgan's disappearance, a farmer taking a load of produce to market happened to glance up to the third-floor attic window of a farmhouse and saw William Morgan looking down at him. Or perhaps—the farmer wasn't sure—it was the ghost of Morgan.

Residents of the Lima area had also heard the rumors of this ghost. I happen to know the owners of the American Hotel, Pat and Rose Reynolds, and filmed part of my documentary there. The hotel has been in the family since 1929, and they had heard many stories about Morgan from family members and customers over the years, including this one. In fact, the Reynolds have known the various owners of the farmhouse over the years and have personally heard reports that footsteps could be heard in the attic some evenings and that the smell of cigar smoke sometimes wafted down into the house from up there.

# The Strange Disappearance of Captain William Morgan

## DEATHBED CONFESSIONS

What happened to Morgan on that night in 1826, when he was released into the hands of his enemies? The mystery has never been solved and probably never will be. But the case is periodically reinvigorated by the discovery of new evidence, new testimony and renewed speculation. Two of the most interesting examples of this were confessions that came on the deathbeds of men who were involved in the case.

In 1848, Henry L. Valance, a Freemason and an alleged participant in the plot, made a deathbed confession to his physician, Dr. John L. Emery. Valance reportedly began by saying: "My last hour is approaching; and as the things of this world fade from my mental sight, I feel the necessity of making, as far as in my power lies, that atonement which every violator of the great law of right owes to his fellow men. I allude to the abduction and murder of the ill-fated William Morgan."[19] A year after Valance died, Emery published an account of the confession in a small pamphlet dedicated solely to the topic. The account is intriguing, especially because it hews so closely to the most widely accepted theory about the fate of Morgan—that is, he had been, in fact, abducted and drowned.

Another deathbed confession of a sort was offered by none other than Thurlow Weed. In this case, however, Weed was confessing not for something he did but for something another person supposedly did. Weed said on his deathbed that John Whitney, who had been convicted on a conspiracy charge related to Morgan's disappearance, had in fact related to him the gruesome details of what actually happened to Morgan. According to Weed, Whitney claimed that five men, including Whitney, had bound Morgan with chains and dumped him in the middle of the Niagara River. Whitney, however, who survived Weed, denied ever making the statement.

## WILLIAM MORGAN'S BONES

The Morgan affair received another round of publicity when a skeleton was discovered on June 22, 1881, in Pembroke, Genesee County. Workmen digging a quarry came upon the skeleton, buried "about three rods" from the road, in a location about two miles south of the Tonawanda Indian Reservation. The bones had been covered with a thick layer of rocks and dirt, testimony to the intentions of those who had buried it there.

Discovered along with the bones was a silver ring engraved with the initials "W.M." Also found was a small tin box that was probably used to keep tobacco and, in it, a piece of paper. The box crumbled to dust as soon as it was touched, but the paper was taken to the office of a local doctor, where it was placed under a microscope: The words "masons, liar, prison, kill, and Henry Brown" were clearly visible on it. It appeared, in other words, to be a threatening note from Henry Brown, a lawyer and Mason, who had publicly defended the Masons against the charge of abducting Morgan in the years immediately following the crime.[20]

In the end, however, it was never proven that the bones were Morgan's. The skeleton was found some fifty years after he disappeared, well before the advent of DNA testing, and long after most of those who had any first-person familiarity with the case were long gone as well.

The location of the bones, however, has a tantalizing correspondence to one final theory about the fate of William Morgan.

## The Wakeman Thesis

Nearly one hundred years after the event, another possible solution to the Morgan mystery was offered by William S. Wakeman. A commercial photographer and the son of a congressman, Wakeman was a Batavia resident who had been adopted by the Seneca Indians and grew up on the Tonawanda Reservation.

In his book, *The William Morgan Mystery Solved*, Wakeman claimed that he had been told the true story of what happened to Morgan, and what is more, that he also had documentary proof of his assertions. Wakeman claimed that he was told the story of Morgan's fate by Chauncey Abrams and Otto Parker, both members of the Tonawanda Band of the Seneca Indians. The story had been handed down to them by General Ely Parker, also a Seneca, a prominent Mason and an attorney, diplomat and engineer as well.

Wakeman's account follows the generally accepted theory until Morgan was brought to Fort Niagara. There, according to Wakeman, Morgan was to have been turned over to some Canadian Indians, who had apparently been given some consideration for taking this problem off the hands of the Masons. But at the last minute, the Indians refused to take part in the affair. Then, according to Wakeman, Colonel King, a Mason, made arrangements to turn Morgan over instead to the Seneca on the Tonawanda Reservation.

# The Strange Disappearance of Captain William Morgan

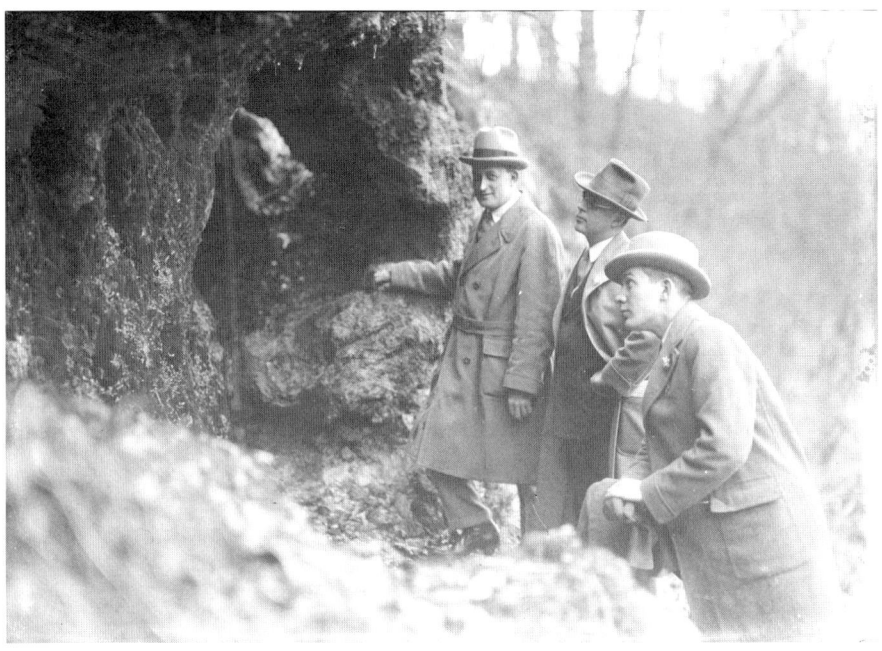

A cave thought to have been used by William Morgan as a hiding place. One theory posits that Morgan engineered his "kidnapping" to boost book sales. *Courtesy of Rochester Public Library.*

Thus Wakeman claims, Morgan was taken to the Seneca reservation—only fifteen miles from his home in Batavia—where he died a natural death three years and one month after his abduction. The reason that Morgan was never discovered living there, maintained Wakeman, was because there was so much internal turmoil on the reservation. At that time, the Seneca were engaged with a fight against the U.S. government because their land was to be taken away from them and they were to be driven to the far west. Thus, anyone could have gone there and lived without fear of discovery. Furthermore, according to Wakeman, Morgan was free to return to Batavia at any time but chose not to in order not to hurt the sale of his book and to avoid his responsibilities to his investors and his family.

Wakeman's theory, like all of the others, continues to be the focus of historical research, investigation and speculation. It seems unlikely at this juncture that anyone will ever know the truth about the strange disappearance of Captain William Morgan.

# CHAPTER 7
# Root Work

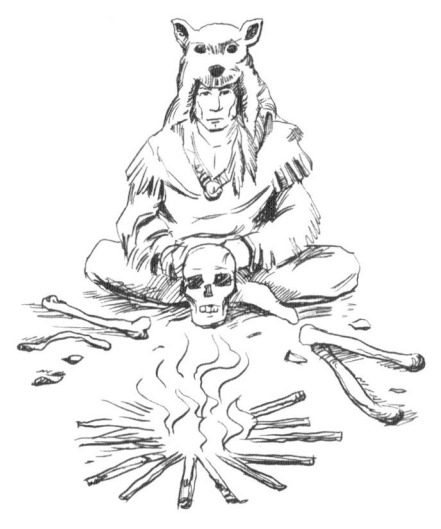

As the story of Captain William Morgan demonstrates, Rochester was becoming a kind of crossroads in American life, a place where many of the issues and problems of the nation as a whole were being played out. This is perhaps especially true in the area of social and religious change. The religious restlessness that impelled the settling of the colonies in the first place had not ended, and this period would witness the development of truly American religious ideas and sects. This period would become known in American history as the Second Great Awakening, and a good portion of it took place in New York—in fact, in an area no larger than a thirty- by thirty-mile stretch along the Erie Canal with the epicenter at Hoodoo Corner. In the early decades of the nineteenth century, many Americans were on the move, and they had a long-established habit of religious freedom, something of an inborn spirit of questioning. With the end of the Revolutionary Wars and the "Indian problem" solved in New York and Pennsylvania, the frontier was shifting ever westward. The Erie

Canal first brought many new laborers into the area, and when it was finished, it brought many travelers as well.

Many people were just passing through. Others perhaps thought they were and then found reason to stay. Many were clearly drawn by the increased demand for labor not only for the canal but also for the new businesses that were formed to support and take advantage of it. This affected the social composition of the area as well. Quickly growing Rochester was drawing not only Americans but recent immigrants as well, with sometimes predictable culture clashes ensuing. The cultural mixing that began with Indians in surrounding areas increased to include more European settlers—primarily Irish and German—and many French Canadians, who came from across Lake Ontario to find work. African Americans began to arrive in the area as well, a topic that will be more fully covered in later chapters.

Some of the most dramatic developments in this period and place were in the area of religion. In fact, the region would become what the historian Emerson Klees termed the Psychic Highway.[21] By this, he meant both traditional Christian ideas, in new forms of organization and emphasis, and also a broader spirit of pursuing meaning in the supernatural, particularly by seeking connection with those who moved beyond the earthly plane. In fact, by the middle of the century, the Rochester area would be the center of a new psychic movement, grounded in some ways by the Fox sisters, whose story we will also explore later.

\*\*\*

The inaugural event of this religious explosion occurred in 1829, when Sam Patch, a daredevil by profession, jumped into the ninety-nine-foot-high falls of the Genesee River. On a cold November day, before a crowd of some 7,500 people, he walked out onto a rock ledge in the middle of the falls and threw his pet bear cub over the falls. The cub managed to swim safely to shore, and then Patch—as if he had received confirmation that the deed was possible—jumped as well. He disappeared beneath the water for a moment, then rose and swam successfully to the other side. The crowd was thrilled.

Although it was by all measures a success, Patch was disappointed with the results of his jump. The weather had been bad, and the turnout was smaller than he'd expected. He'd therefore raised far less money than he'd hoped, and Patch was hoping to earn a living with his daredevil skills. A Rhode

Islander by birth, Patch had begun working in a cotton mill as a child. He'd acquired a reputation as a jumper while still a child, when he entertained other boys by jumping off the mill dam. By his early twenties, he was still working at a mill, though he began traveling and jumping from higher and more dangerous spots. He was finally beginning to attract crowds. In 1827, he jumped off the seventy-foot Passaic Falls in New Jersey, and in 1828, he jumped one hundred feet at Hoboken, New Jersey, thus acquiring his moniker "Patch the New Jersey Jumper." In 1829, he acquired national fame by leaping into the Niagara River near the base of Niagara Falls. At that point, his name became a household word, and his slogan, "Some things can be done as well as others," became a popular expression.

So Patch decided that he would repeat his feat on the Genesee, hoping for better weather, a bigger crowd and perhaps better press. A few days later, on Friday, November 13, he got his wish: a crowd of ten thousand gathered, with plenty of journalists present, to watch him repeat the jump. This time, he increased the height of the jump to 125 feet by constructing a 25-foot stand on the rock ledge. It may have been a fatal mistake. Some accounts of the event suggest that he fell from the stand rather than jumped, but in any case, he did not perform his usual feet-first vertical entry. There was the sound of a loud impact, attested to by many observers, and then Patch disappeared beneath the water, never to surface again.

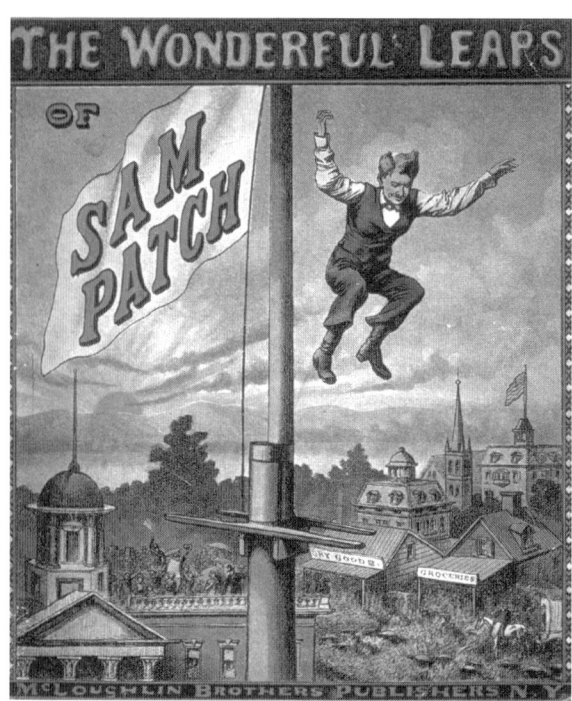

An illustration depicting daredevil Sam Patch. His fatal leap in 1829 is believed to have served as a catalyst for revivalism in Rochester. *Courtesy of Rochester Public Library.*

Although many people believed that Patch had died upon impact or perhaps even before, given the description of the jump, or drowned, many also believed widely circulated rumors that the disappearance was, in fact, part of the stunt. Patch, it was claimed, had hidden in a cave at the base of the falls and was then taken away by coconspirators. He was, according to this line of thinking, now in hiding, enjoying the fuss he'd created. But the rumors were put to rest the following spring when Patch's frozen body was found in the ice near Rochester.

Some local ministers and newspapers were quick to blame the crowd, calling into the question the moral role of the spectators. This tone of judgment is apparent in even the first reporting on the event, and it only increased with confirmation of Patch's death. Had Patch been drinking? Who might have known or might have stopped him? Had the presence of the spectators played a role? Had their curiosity driven him to be reckless or careless? Where did the blame lie? And most crucially, was this event a symptom of wider social degradation?

Such moral questions were taken up in the churches and began drawing preachers and ministers to the area, ushering in the revivalist movement.

One such revivalist was Charles Grandison Finney (1792–1875), who is sometimes called the father of modern revivalism. Born in Connecticut, the son of a farmer, he first studied law in upstate New York. But on a walk one day, pondering a biblical passage, he underwent a life-changing event. He later wrote, "It seemed as if I met the Lord Jesus Christ face to face…I fell down at His feet and poured out my soul to Him…the Holy Spirit descended upon me in a manner that seemed to go through me, body and soul."[22] Finney soon abandoned the study of law and became a licensed minister in the Presbyterian Church. Rather than taking up responsibility for a congregation, however, he found himself drawn to itinerate evangelism, to preaching among westward-moving pioneer families.

He was one of the first preachers to speak extemporaneously, relying not on a prepared text but speaking from the heart. He led a series of revivals in upstate New York and also in places like Boston and Philadelphia, and the period became known as Finney's "Nine Mighty Years of Evangelism." Revivalism was a movement that emphasized a returning to religion and contained within it the notion of being "born again." The style of these churches and events were more emotional, more free-flowing than traditional ones.

The Rochester Revival of 1830 eclipsed all others. Finney was invited to preach by the wife of a prominent Rochester attorney, who had apparently issued the invitation more out of a sense of duty than feeling, for she worried to a friend that Finney might bring in a revival that would ruin the social season. But Finney's preaching reached her personally, for during Finney's

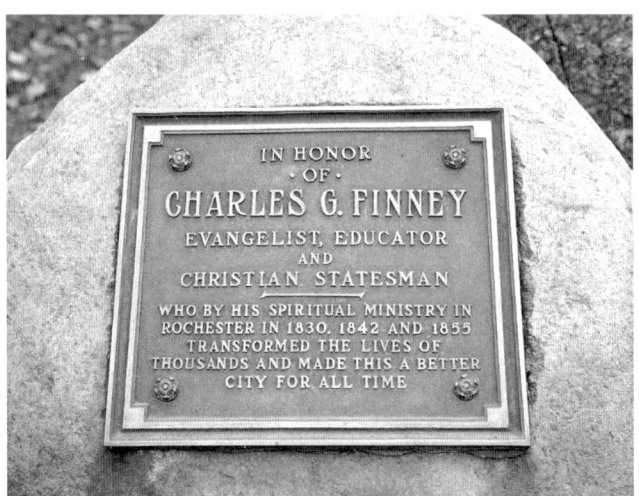

A plaque in honor of Charles G. Finney, 1792–1875, a prominent evangelist who preached widely in western New York.

sermon, the "woman fell to her knees, wracked with sobs." It was a crucial moment for Finney, and for the movement as a whole. Finney later wrote: "It was soon seen that the Lord was aiming at the conversion of the highest classes of society. My meetings soon became thronged with that class…As the revival swept through the town, and converted the great mass of the most influential people, both men and women; the change in the order, sobriety, and morality of the city was wonderful."[23]

Thus the Second Great Awakening was launched, a period of nationwide religious renewal. But one of the most remarkable things is that so many of these developments can be traced to such a relatively small geographic region. There are various ways to describe the geography in which these developments were contained. Emerson Klees, for instance, traces the developments to a "narrow band of New York State from southwest Buffalo to Albany along the Erie Canal." Another historian, Carl Carmer, says the locus is a "hilly strip scarcely twenty-five miles wide of rolling land from east of Albany to west of Buffalo."[24] It is clear that the Erie Canal itself was a crucial factor in bringing so many of these people into the area in this period, though there are some significant developments that predate the completion of the canal as well.

In fact, the entire state was an incredibly rich and active environment, the religious movements startling in sheer number and variety. Older, more established denominations like the Society of Friends (Quakers) and Shakers were undergoing change, while newer sects like the Baptists were growing at a fast pace. And brand-new groups like the Oneida Community, the Millerites, the Harrisites and the Latter-day Saints were emerging.

# Root Work

## Joseph Smith and the Church of Jesus Christ of Latter-Day Saints

One of the most remarkable religious developments of this period was the birth of a new, wholly American religion, one that is today the fastest growing church on earth: the Church of Jesus Christ of Latter-day Saints. Events began in 1820, with a series of visions by a young man who lived in the town of Palmyra, some twenty miles west of Rochester.

Joseph Smith (1805–1844) was born in Vermont to a migrant farming couple. The Smiths, by all accounts, had economic difficulties during Joseph's childhood. They moved frequently, as a consequence of both crop failures and ill-fated business ventures. The family lived a difficult life. During the winter of Joseph's eighth year, his leg became dangerously infected. Some doctors reportedly advised amputation, but the family refused. The boy underwent a successful operation to remove part of his shin bone (without anesthesia or the then most commonly used tranquilizer, whiskey). Joseph eventually recovered, although he used crutches for several years and limped for the rest of his life.

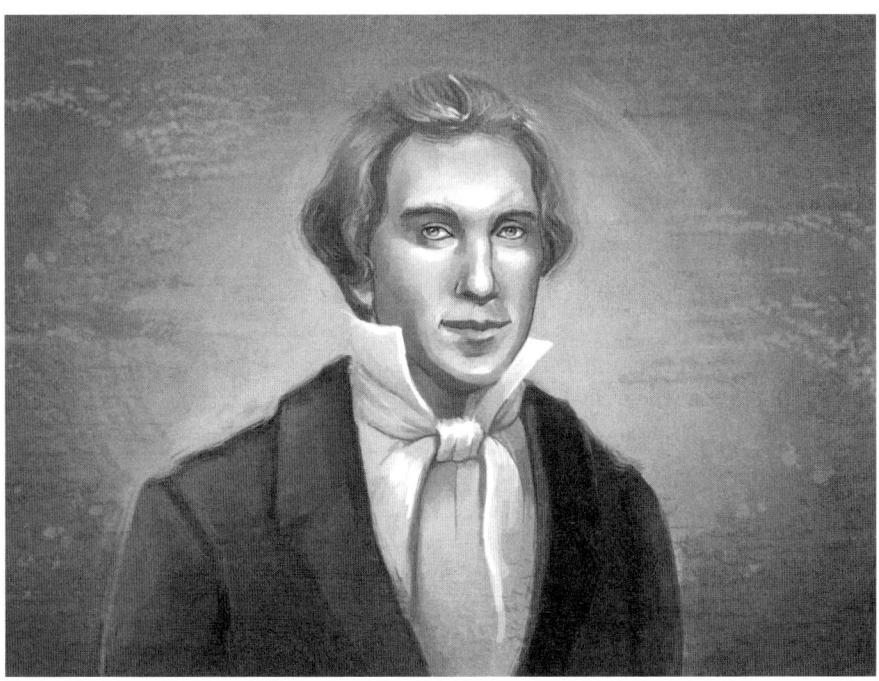

An illustration of Joseph Smith, 1805–1844, founder of the Mormon Church and publisher of the *Book of Mormon*.

In 1816 or 1817 (the evidence is unclear), the Smith family was reportedly "warned out of" the town in Vermont in which they were living. They had been moving from town to town, seeking work, and this was then a commonly used method in New England for communities to pressure "outsiders" to settle elsewhere and can probably be traced to the family's financial difficulties. At any rate, the family left New England, moving to the village of Palmyra. For three years, the father and elder sons worked odd jobs and squatted in a log home until they were able to obtain a mortgage for a one-hundred-acre farm in the nearby town of Manchester.

The Smith family does not appear to have been extraordinarily religious. There is no evidence that they regularly attended church, but Joseph did participate in some church events as a youth. There is some conflicting evidence about whether he regularly read the Bible as a child, although his mother seemed to indicate that he did not do so until his late teens. With his family, he took part in religious folk magic, which was then a common practice but one that many Christian clergymen condemned. Like many people in that era, the family believed in Christian mysticism, and both Joseph's parents and his maternal grandfather had visions and dreams that they believed communicated messages from God.

Smith's own first vision occurred in the spring, during a walk in the woods. It was, he later said, the first time that he had attempted to pray. He kneeled, he said, and "began to offer up the desires of my heart to God." The account continues:

> *I had scarcely done so, when immediately I was seized upon by some power which entirely overcame me, and had such an astonishing influence over me as to bind my tongue so that I could not speak. Thick darkness gathered around me, and it seemed to me for a time as if I were doomed to sudden destruction. But, exerting all my powers to call upon God to deliver me out of the power of this enemy which had seized upon me, and at the very moment when I was ready to sink into despair and abandon myself to destruction—not to an imaginary ruin, but to the power of some actual being from the unseen world, who had such marvelous power as I had never before felt in any being—just at this moment of great alarm, I saw a pillar of light exactly over my head, above the brightness of the sun, which descended gradually until it fell upon me…It no sooner appeared than I found myself delivered from the enemy which held me bound.*

# Root Work

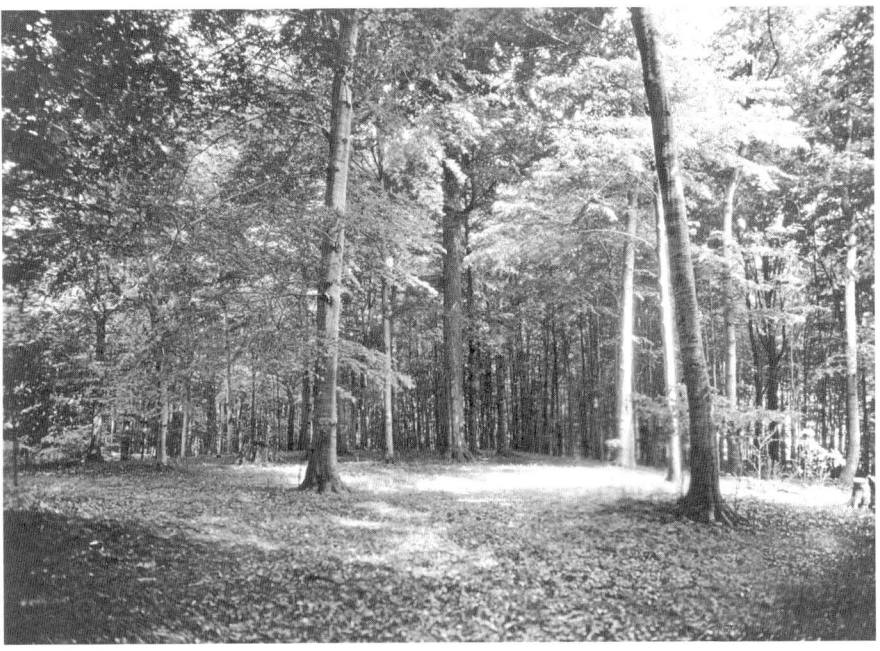

A view of the area in Palmyra, New York, that is known as the Sacred Grove, where Mormons believe Joseph Smith received a vision of God in 1820. *Courtesy of Rochester Public Library.*

Though this vision might have had an immediate and profound effect on Smith, it was some time before it became the guiding force of his life. He'd had very little formal schooling and filled his time by working on his father's farm, hunting, fishing, taking odds jobs and pursuing small business ventures (e.g., selling cake and beer at public events). Smith was described by contemporaries as quiet, even taciturn, and though good-natured, he wasn't given to laughing. In 1822, the Smiths began building a frame house located on the property that they owned. In November 1823, Joseph's older brother Alvin died. By 1825, the Smiths were unable to make their final mortgage payment, and the house and farm were foreclosed on. Desperate, the family persuaded a neighbor, Lemuel Durfee, to buy the farm, and they rented it back from him.

One way in which the Smith family supplemented its meager farm income was by treasure digging. This was a relatively common activity in this period. Joseph, in particular, claimed a special ability to use "seer" stones for locating lost items and buried treasure. He would apparently put a stone in a white stovepipe hat and then receive information about the location of items in reflections given off by the stone. It was believed that a treasure seeker maintained his powers by being sexually pure, and this appears to have had a profound effect on Smith.

In 1823, perhaps while praying to be purified from a sexual sin, Smith said he was visited at night by an angel named Moroni, who revealed that there was a cache of items hidden in a hill named Cumorah. The cache included a buried book made of golden plates, a breastplate and a set of silver spectacles with lenses composed of seer stones. Smith later reported that he attempted to remove the golden plates the next morning, but he was unable to do so because the angel struck him down with force, saying that the tablets could only be removed when Smith was accompanied to Cumorah by the "right person."

Over the next few years, Smith made annual visits to Cumorah but returned each time without the golden plates, because the angel was dissatisfied in some way by the people he had with him. Smith would later say that his brother Alvin was, in fact, the "right person," but by the time Joseph figured that out, Alvin had died. At any rate, Smith continued to travel western New York and Pennsylvania as a treasure hunter, even being arrested and tried in 1826 as a "disorderly person" for these activities. In 1827, he met a young woman named Emma Hale and eloped with her because her parents disapproved of the match.

Believing that Emma would satisfy the angel as the "right person," Smith went with her to Cumorah on September 22, 1827. This time, he successfully retrieved the plates and placed them in a locked chest. He refused to allow anyone, including his family, to view the plates directly, saying that the angel had commanded him not to show the plates but only to publish a translation of them. Smith reportedly kept the plates in a chest under the hearth in his parents' home and later moved them under the floor boards of his parents' old log home nearby. He also reported that, at one point, he took the plates out of the chest, left the empty chest under the floor boards and hid the plates in a barrel of flax. It appears that Smith was particularly concerned about the safety of the plates because he was involved in a dispute with other treasure hunters, who accused him of double-crossing them and taking for himself what was rightly joint property. Some dozen of them ransacked his hiding places, looking for stolen loot and/or the golden plates. Smith is said to have realized that he could not accomplish the translation of the golden plates in Palmyra. He took a loan of fifty dollars from a neighbor, paid his debts in Palmyra and then moved with his wife to Harmony Township, Pennsylvania.

That neighbor might be counted as the first of Smith's religious followers. The man had agreed to the loan after hefting the chest said to contain the plates, and he professed a belief in Smith's mission. Smith began to build a following as news of the golden plates spread. The plates, Smith said, described the religious history of American indigenous peoples. In March 1830, Smith published a translation from the "reformed Egyptian" of the golden plates, titled *The Book of Mormon: An Account Written by the Hand of Mormon upon Plates Taken from the Plates of Nephi*. *The Book of Mormon* is divided into smaller books, titled after individuals named as primary authors and, in most versions, divided into chapters and verses. The English is very similar to the early modern English style of the King James version of the Bible. The original manuscript reportedly ran to some 532 pages and was one long sentence. It took the editor three months to punctuate it!

In 1830, Smith organized the first Church of Jesus Christ of Latter-day Saints, claiming it was a restoration of the true church of Jesus Christ, from which other churches had strayed due to a Great Apostasy. Smith also left the region that year, taking the majority of his church members to Kirtland, Ohio. He sent another group to Jackson County, Missouri, in an attempt to establish a city of Zion there, as the biblical New Jerusalem. But Smith's plans for Zion were repeatedly frustrated. In 1833, Missouri settlers expelled the Latter-day Saints (LDS) from Jackson County, and Smith's paramilitary campaign to redeem the area was unsuccessful. Smith turned his attention to Kirtland and undertook the construction of an expensive temple there. But in early 1838, after a financial scandal effectively caused the collapse of the Ohio church, Smith fled an arrest warrant and joined those of his followers who remained in Missouri. When many of the Kirtland Saints followed him to Missouri, tensions escalated with non-LDS settlers, leading to open warfare.

The Saints were expelled from Missouri, and in 1839, Smith and his followers settled in Nauvoo, Illinois. Smith learned from previous instances in which the presence of the Mormons became unacceptable to residents of an area and sought to ground the presence of the church in secular authority as well. He became the mayor of the town and commander of the Nauvoo Legion, a sizeable branch of the Illinois militia. He also directed the construction of a second temple. In 1843, Smith formally introduced a number of changes in the church, including "plural marriage, the eternal progression of man toward godhood, eternalizing of the marriage covenant, the endowment ceremony, and the political kingdom of God with its secret Council of Fifty."[25]

Some members of the church raised objections. The group included Smith's second counselor and one of the presidents of the Nauvoo Stake and several business and professional people. They were excommunicated from the Church in April 1844. They then purchased a printing press and began publishing a newspaper, the *Nauvoo Expositor*. The paper made a number of charges against Smith: that he was a tyrant, and that he had introduced into the church doctrine and practices that were contrary to the original teachings of the church. On June 7, they exposed the practice of polygamy within the church, calling it "whoredoms and abominations," and accused Smith of being behind it.[26] The stage was now set for the last act of Smith's life.

The *Nauvoo Expositor* subsequently published another article announcing Smith's intention to repeal the city charter, and argued against it, saying that the city should be governed in accordance with principles of the separation of church and state. The following morning and the Monday thereafter, the city council and Mayor Joseph Smith met to consider the problem. They termed the charges against Smith a threat to the peace and security of the city and used their power to declare the newspaper a nuisance. Smith, in effect, declared martial law in the city. The government of the State of Illinois then got involved, accusing Smith of treason. He was arrested and jailed.

But before a trial could be held, a mob of about two hundred armed men stormed the jail on the afternoon of June 27, 1844. Smith tried to defend

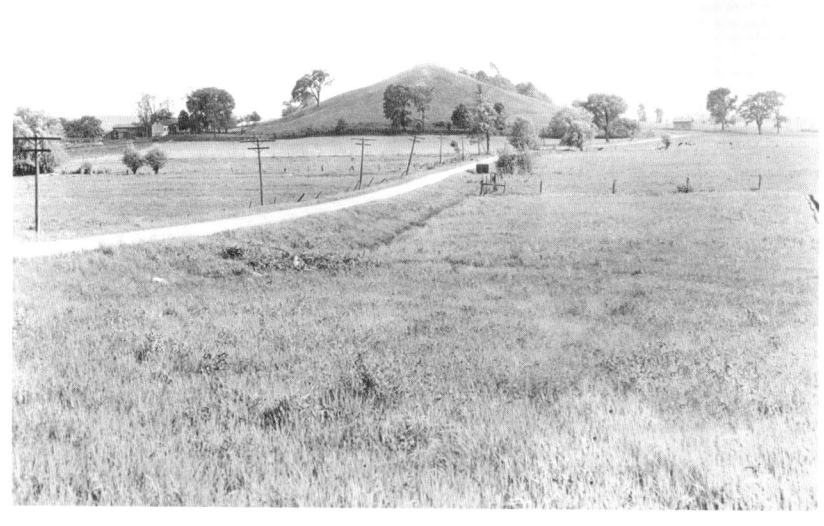

The site known as Hill Cumorah, where Joseph Smith claimed to have found golden plates detailing the history of early Native Americans. *Courtesy of Rochester Public Library.*

himself with a small pistol that had been smuggled in to him, to no avail. He ran out of ammunition, and some of the men broke into the cell. Joseph Smith turned to make his way toward the window to jump and was shot twice in the back and hit a third time in the chest by a bullet fired from a musket on the ground outside. His body fell out of the window. Some accounts suggest that Smith was alive when he hit the ground and was further abused by the crowd—perhaps even propped against a wall and executed—though the best evidence suggests he was in fact dead when he hit the ground, and that his body was then mutilated by the crowd.

Two years later, Brigham Young began the Mormon exodus to Utah.

Though much of Smith's story takes place outside our central geographic area of interest, it has been told in some detail because many of its themes are strikingly similar to those of this work. Like Handsome Lake, Joseph Smith had a vision that would change not only his own life but the course of history of "his" people. Smith developed his ideas in the same environment that was shaping other religious thinkers. Like Charles Finney, John Humphrey Noyes, William Miller and many other preachers and ministers in this period and place, Smith used the body of Christian knowledge and practice to craft a religion in his own particular way. And like the others, many of Smith's earliest followers came off the "psychic highway" and found a new religious home.

By the late 1840s, religious activity in the region was waning, and it then acquired a new moniker: the Burned-Over District. As a largely agricultural people knew, a wildfire cannot burn without fuel, and the phrase brilliantly captures this idea, that the religious flames had burned so fiercely in the area that they, eventually, consumed all the fuel. As Winthrop S. Hudson, a historian of religion commented, "The first half of the nineteenth century in the United States was a time of eager expectancy, unbridled enthusiasm, and restless ferment. A new nation and a new world was being born, and to many anything and everything were possible. It was a period when a comet's tail was said to have swept America, and everyone went a little mad."[27] By midcentury, the religious fires were burning out. There were no more people to be saved, no more people who had energy to give to new denominations, new ideas and new theologies.

\*\*\*

Set against the backdrop of rather extreme religious developments such as Millerism, the Oneida Community and the beginnings of Mormonism, we have paid rather less attention to the growth during this period of more traditional, or mainstream, Christian denominations or splits within them, but this was happening as well. While revivalism and religious fervor played a role in these developments, other issues were in play as well. Particularly, as the 1820s gave over to the 1830s, social concerns—especially the role of women and the issue of slavery—became more prominent.

Questions about the moral condition of slavery had always been a part of American life, but they were beginning to acquire a new urgency in this period. In 1831, for instance, Nat Turner, a slave and Baptist preacher, led a slave rebellion in Virginia that resulted in the death of nearly sixty white men, women and children. It was a moment that deeply shocked the south and many in the north as well. Following this, Virginia passed a law requiring black congregations to meet only in the presence of a white minister. Other states restricted exclusively black churches or passed laws regulating the assembly of blacks in large groups unsupervised by whites, which had the same effect. There were, likewise, political battles being waged in national institutions, and the abolition movement was beginning in earnest. Many Baptists, in particular, found themselves on the front lines in respect to these questions.

In Rochester, the First Baptist Church was formed in 1818 with thirteen members. Initially, it met in a room above the Clinton House Inn. In 1828, the congregation moved into the first church built in the city, a former Presbyterian Church, which was constructed in 1818 and located on Fitzhugh Street. By 1834, the congregation had grown to 373 members, thanks largely to the work of Charles Finney. The congregation was too large for the church building, and so letters of dismissal—effectively, leave to create a new congregation—were issued to fifty-three members.[28]

Those members then established the Second Baptist Church of Rochester as a "church of, for, and by the people who heard Jesus gladly." It was founded on March 12, 1834, meeting initially at the home of one of its members. The first pastor of the church, Elon Galusha (1790–1856), was the son of Jonas Galusha, a governor of Vermont. He was a Millerite as well as a Baptist and would remain active in the Millerite movement until its collapse in 1845. But one of the primary motivating forces for Galusha was his opposition to slavery. In 1940, he served as the first president of the National Baptist Anti-Slavery Convention, founded the Baptist Anti-Slavery Society and represented the American and Foreign Anti-Slavery Society at the World Anti-Slavery Convention. These activities provoked the Southern Baptists to exclude him from the American Board of Commissioners for Foreign Missions.[29]

In 1834, the Second Baptist Church bought the former Third Presbyterian Church at the corner of Main and Clinton Streets, adjacent to our Hoodoo Corner. Significantly, the Second Baptist Church was also the first church in Rochester, and perhaps in the entire country, that allowed blacks to become members and to worship openly with whites.[30] It would eventually become a way station on the Underground Railroad[31] and a symbol for the home the abolitionist movement would find in Rochester.

The state of New York was a hotbed of abolitionist activity. The city of Utica was the first to hold a statewide Anti-Slavery Convention in 1835. And the next year, an antislavery society was founded in Rochester. This association with abolitionism and black culture, in general, provides another key to the legend of Hoodoo Corner. Rochester would become a key location in the abolitionist movement. By 1847, Frederick Douglass, the most prominent African American of his time, had settled in the city. This gives us another clue as to the origins—or perhaps more precisely, the persistence—of the term Hoodoo Corner. If there was already some idea of a jinx and an "otherness" attached to this geographic point—if the presence of an Indian burial ground and the rumors that Captain William Morgan might have spent his last night here at the Farmers' Tavern and Inn—then those ideas were about to be solidified by further developments in the area, including the first murder in Rochester, very near Hoodoo Corner.

## CHAPTER 8
# The Murder of William Lyman

At approximately 9:00 p.m., William Lyman closed up the office at the Rochester Railroad Company where he worked and set off down the street toward his home. Lyman, a devoted family man and diligent employee, was employed by the J.W. Hooker Mill as a purchasing agent, dealing in wheat commodities. In this capacity, Lyman frequently handled large cash transactions and, as was his custom, carried a large bundle of cash home with him for 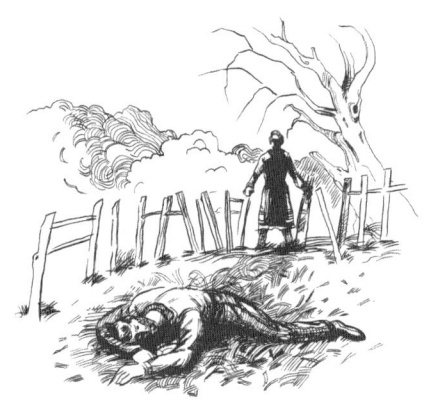 the evening. It was to be deposited in the bank the following morning on his way to work.

Lyman had apparently not noticed (or, if he had, he had apparently not been alarmed by) the man, it would later be reported, who was seen loitering around outside the railroad office all day.

Lyman took his customary path home, walking through the streets of his adopted city, Rochester. Born into a prominent colonial family in Massachusetts, Lyman had moved to the city with his wife, Amanda, in the early 1820s. As had so many others, he had been drawn by the economic potential of the city. Lyman, like many able and ambitious men in that period, had come to take work in the industry that was fueling much of that

## The Murder of William Lyman

growth, such as the trade in foodstuffs and other natural resources along the Erie Canal.

As Lyman neared his home on Clinton Street, located a short distance from Hoodoo Corner, he took a shortcut into an open alley that would allow him easy access to his house. The alley was unlit. As Lyman took the last few paces toward his home, the man who had been following him made his move, creeping up behind Lyman and shooting once into the back of his head, killing him instantly.

It was October 20, 1837, and William Lyman, age thirty-seven and the father of four young children, had just become the first murder victim in Rochester history.

\* \* \*

But it just so happened that these two men were not the only people in the area at the time of the shooting. Thomas Dixon, just nine years old, was also nearby. According to the witness statement he later gave to police, he was heading toward his own home on a course that took him by the Second Baptist Church, located at the intersection of Clinton and Main Streets, roughly one block from Hoodoo Corner. Dixon reported that he heard the 9:00 p.m. bell, and a few minutes later when he got to the fence by Franklin Street, he was "alarmed by the sounds of footsteps" near him. He paused, heard a shot and saw a flash as the gun discharged. Believing that he had witnessed a man shooting a dog that had been barking—and frightened by the man with the gun, who wore a "shiny hat" and who then "bent down" over something—Dixon turned and ran home.

Amanda Lyman also heard the gun discharge. She went to the window and drew back the curtain, looking out, but she saw nothing. She also knew, she told the police, that when her husband hadn't arrived home by 9:10 p.m. to take his evening tea, that something was wrong. But neither Dixon nor Amanda Lyman took any further action that evening. The city went to sleep as usual, not yet knowing that one of its prominent, upstanding citizens had been murdered.

Early the next morning, when Dixon awoke, he made his way to the yard where he had seen the flash of light and heard the shot the night before. He expected to find the body of a dog, but he was shocked to see "someone lying in the field," so he went home, told his father and showed him "where

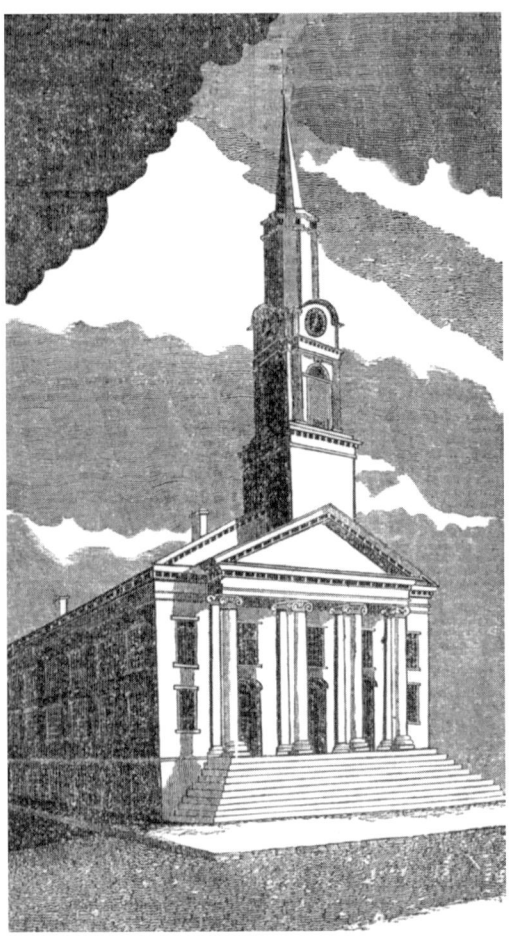

An illustration of the Second Baptist Church, located one block from Main and Elm Streets, where nine-year-old Thomas Dixon heard the shot that killed William Lyman. *Courtesy of Rochester Public Library.*

the man was." Or such was the testimony that Dixon gave during the trial of the man who would eventually be convicted of Lyman's murder. It should be noted, though, that Dixon's testimony at trial, and in the immediate aftermath of the event, was somewhat different. When he testified at the indictment proceedings, roughly a week after the murder, the boy added details. He claimed that, upon discovering the body, he noticed that "a package wrapped in brown paper lay near the hat, close to where the blood showed that the victim had dropped when shot." Dixon "placed the package in the hat, and set the hat beside the head of the body." He then "told some other boys of the corpse, and they went to rouse the neighbors," before Dixon finally decided to go get his father.

And although the precise detail—whether Dixon touched the hat and the package or not (there was not yet any concept of scientific analysis of a crime scene, so the boy cannot be faulted for contaminating it) and then went to get his father or simply told some neighborhood boys about the body—isn't significant historically, it does point to one of the difficulties in reconstructing traumatic events, especially when they are historic episodes such as this. There are some discrepancies in the accounts of this crime in the sources, particularly between what a witness says early on and then says later.

# The Murder of William Lyman

Nevertheless, the language of the participants in the trial—the lawyers, judge, witnesses—is remarkable. The language was unique and rich, descriptive and emotional. In such circumstances, it seems best to allow the participants to speak for themselves whenever possible and simply make note of the discrepancies between individuals or the same individual at various times. It is the best way to tell the story as it was lived by the participants.[32]

## "Outrage Unparalleled in Rochester—Assassination!"

### Daily Advertiser, *October 30, 1837*

By 7:00 a.m., neighbors and passersby were gathering in the area just behind Lyman's house to observe the body, lying face down, stiff and cold. There was a one-inch bullet wound behind Lyman's right ear. The location of blood and the marks on the ground suggested that Lyman's body had been dragged a few feet from where he initially fell. His outerwear had been removed, and his pockets had been turned inside out. Lyman's wallet and another small satchel were missing. Both of those were believed to contain money, estimated to be a few hundred paper dollars, and a few gold coins. The package that had been found lying near his hat was found to contain $5,000 in Connecticut River Banking Company money. The killer or killers had apparently missed it. Within minutes of the discovery, an alarm was issued. Word spread quickly through town, and rewards for information about the murder were immediately posted.

Robert King, the sheriff of Monroe County, arrived quickly with a team of eleven men and took charge of the investigation. He wasted no time in interviewing Dixon, whose description of the "shiny hat" immediately became the most important clue. Only one kind of man wore a shiny cap—or a "glazed" cap, as it was also known—and that was a foreigner who worked on the canal or in the mills. It was well known that these men congregated on the east side of State Street, which was a collection of nine-pin alleys, low saloons and disorderly houses (i.e., brothels).

King immediately dispatched men to question people who lived in the area. A second piece of crucial information quickly emerged. It came from Hannah Chamberlain, a waitress who worked in a pub near State Street. She reported that, upon getting off work the previous evening, "something caught my eye down on the first floor, where the tavern is." She noticed, she said, "three men sitting at a table with a pile of money between them. They were talking in loud whispers, and looking all around. The one who was doing most of the talking seemed pretty pleased with himself, because he ordered brandies all around." She had seen him there before, she noted, and she thought that he was called "Barron." And, she continued, "I don't know anything about him, except he wears one of those glazed caps."

Sheriff King later recalled:

> It didn't take us long to locate the Barron house, as they were well-known. I spoke to Mrs. Margaret Barron, who said she had a son named Octavius. She didn't know his whereabouts, and had not seen him since yesterday. The young man, age 18, was not unknown to the police, or to the people of Rochester. He was French Canadian, a part-time barge worker, and a petty thief. It was common knowledge that he frequented the taverns and alleys of State Street, and that he usually lived with his mother in the Bowery, not far from where Lyman was murdered.

Providentially, once Sheriff King had secured that crucial piece of information—that Barron had not been home the previous evening—he was

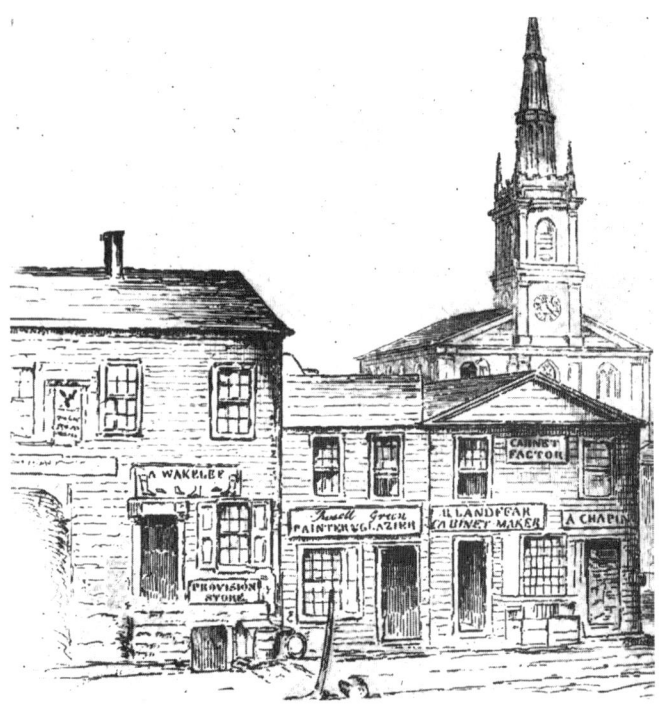

Illustration of the Bowery, two blocks from Main and Elm Streets. The area is where French Canadian immigrants lived, including Octavius Barron. *Courtesy of Rochester Public Library.*

# The Murder of William Lyman

"informed that someone at the train depot had reported a suspicious person lurking there, and as it was only a few blocks away, we went to investigate."

Sheriff King continued:

> *When we arrived at the depot, a Mr. Buckland from New York, who had just arrived on the 8:30 am train, said he had seen someone who had appeared in an unusual hurry, considering the time of day. When we began to search the area, we saw a man kneeling behind a wood pile. Stuck in this woodpile was a handkerchief, with bank notes rolled up inside. When we emptied the pockets of this person, we found more bank notes that seemed to match those in the handkerchief, as well as three gold coins. When questioned, the man said he was going to Buffalo to look for a job. His name was Octavius Barron. I put the cuffs on him and took him to jail.*

Further investigation soon enough determined the identities of the two men in the bar with Barron the previous evening: Leon Fluett and Thomas Bennet. They were quickly arrested as accomplices to the crime. Fewer than twelve hours after the murder, the perpetrator was in custody and would never see freedom again. Barron was quickly and easily arraigned—the evidence against him was overwhelming—and he was sent to Sing-Sing Prison to await trial.

## THE TRIAL

Barron was returned to Monroe County just before his trial began on May 28, 1838. The murder and subsequent trial were the biggest spectacle in Rochester since the disappearance of Captain William Morgan nearly a decade before, and thus the subject of highly detailed newspaper coverage, including verbatim transcription of some witness testimony. The courthouse was packed to capacity with spectators anxious to learn every detail of the crime, and catch a glimpse of the killer, on each of the ten days of the trial.

The trial was presided over by Judge Charles Wentworth, a man known for his oratory, no-nonsense approach to jurisprudence and strict adherence to the law. He had once convicted a man of lewdness for kissing his girlfriend in public.

The opposing lawyers were also well known in the community and well respected for their legal abilities. Curiously, both were also well-known abolitionists. The defense counsel was particularly concerned that the civil rights of Octavius Barron, a French Canadian immigrant, be protected. The murder and ensuing publicity had seemed to release the simmering anger many townspeople felt over immigrants, particularly French Canadians, who were overwhelmingly Catholic. There was religious bigotry in the air. Such social tensions were entirely predictable in a city undergoing rapid growth such as Rochester—the population had doubled in just the previous decade. Thus, many French Canadian workers in the town felt generally, but especially during this period, that they were unwelcome residents of the city. And, in addition to the issue of Barron's national origin and religion, there was the issue of his age. Barely eighteen at the time of the crime, there were some who hoped for, and many more who opposed, a death-penalty pardon on that basis.

The prosecutor, Ashley Sampson, lived in Pittsford in a fine house on Main Street. The house still stands to this day and still contains an original secret door, behind which he hid runaway slaves before they were taken farther north to escape across the river to Canada. Sampson made diligent use of his oratorical skills throughout the trial, as indicated in this excerpt from his opening statement:

> *Every moment's reflection adds to the horror of the deed. The murderer must have been a cool, deliberate villain. The whole bloody scene seems to bear the impress of cautious design, and we doubt not that when all of the facts are developed, it will be found to be the most diabolical offense to darken our fair corporation. The people will show that Octavius Barron hid in the shadows of Mr. Lyman's office on the evening of October 20 last, as he began his journey home…As the poor Mr. Lyman approached his abode on Clinton Place, Mr. Barron crept up behind him and viciously shot him in the head, killing him outright. Quickly taking what he found in Mr. Lyman's pockets, and neglecting to discover the much larger sum of money that Mr. Lyman was protecting under his hat, Barron then joined his friends to celebrate his new-found wealth. After a night of drinking and debauchery, Barron convinced his associates to bring his belongings to the railroad station, for his planned escape.*
>
> *We found Mr. Lyman's money on Barron. We will prove that others saw him following that night. We will prove his alibi to be nothing but lies. And we will prove without a doubt that Octavius Barron is the wanton and depraved killer of William Lyman. You must find him guilty!*

# The Murder of William Lyman

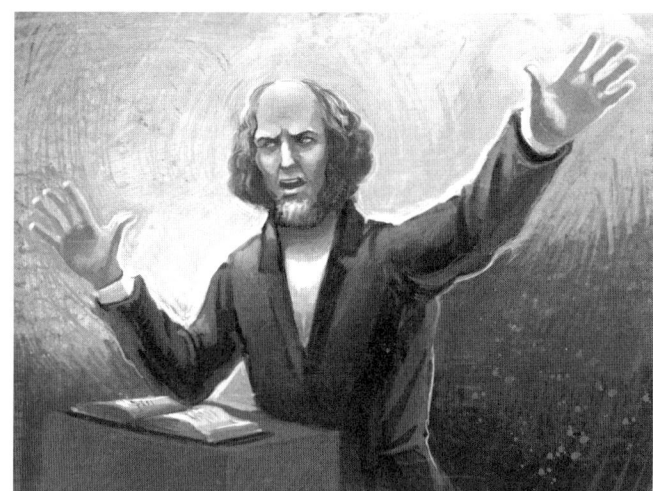

An illustration of Ashley Sampson, 1798–1873, prosecutor in the Lyman murder case. Sampson, an ardent abolitionist, maintained a safe house for escaped slaves in his Pittsford home.

The witness list included forty people, six of whom were able to place Barron in crucial locations on the night of the murder: four who saw Barron loitering outside Lyman's office, and two who saw Barron following Lyman on his walk home that night.

Perhaps the most eagerly anticipated witness was one who had not seen Barron at all on the night of the murder: Margaret Barron, his mother. Under questioning, she refuted the alibi Octavius had given the police—that he was home, asleep at the time of the crime. She steadfastly refuted the assertion, never wavering, stating outright that he hadn't spent the night at home. She also identified the handkerchief containing the dead man's money as belonging to her son.

Throughout the trial, Barron was demonized by the prosecutor and witnesses alike, referred to as a devil and miscreant. It was suggested time and again that Barron's path in life was already set—he was a petty thief, habitual gambler, drinker and carouser—and there was no hope he would ever escape his criminal ways. Barron nonetheless stuck resolutely to his plea of not guilty.

The defense lawyer had little at his disposal with which to work. Barron owned and customarily wore a shiny glazed cap. His own mother refuted his alibi. There was no credible reason given for Barron to be in possession of Lyman's money and gold coins.

There were, however, three critical questions that were not answered by trial testimony: first, the role of Barron's accomplices, Fluett and Bennet; second, the provenance and disposition of the murder weapon; and third, the whereabouts of Barron on the night of the murder, after he was seen by

Chamberlain, the pub waitress, and before he was apprehended at the train station the next morning.

Barron's accomplices were scheduled to go on trial after him. The question of their culpability and punishment would be answered in the last, and perhaps most dramatic, act of this story, as would the second question. But it is the answer to the third question that is most intriguing in the context of this work, because it appears that Barron might have spent the hours between the murder of Lyman and his arrest the next morning in the Farmers' Tavern and Inn.

As mentioned previously, the Farmers' Tavern and Inn was one of the first buildings to go up on the corner of Main and Elm, or Hoodoo Corner. As in the case of Captain William Morgan, there were rumors that the criminals, in both cases, spent the hours immediately following their crimes in this establishment, fortifying themselves with food and drink and perhaps waiting out the hours when they supposed that they might most urgently be sought by authorities. The historical record on this matter is inconclusive, but the persistence of the rumors about Barron's and Morgan's last hours of

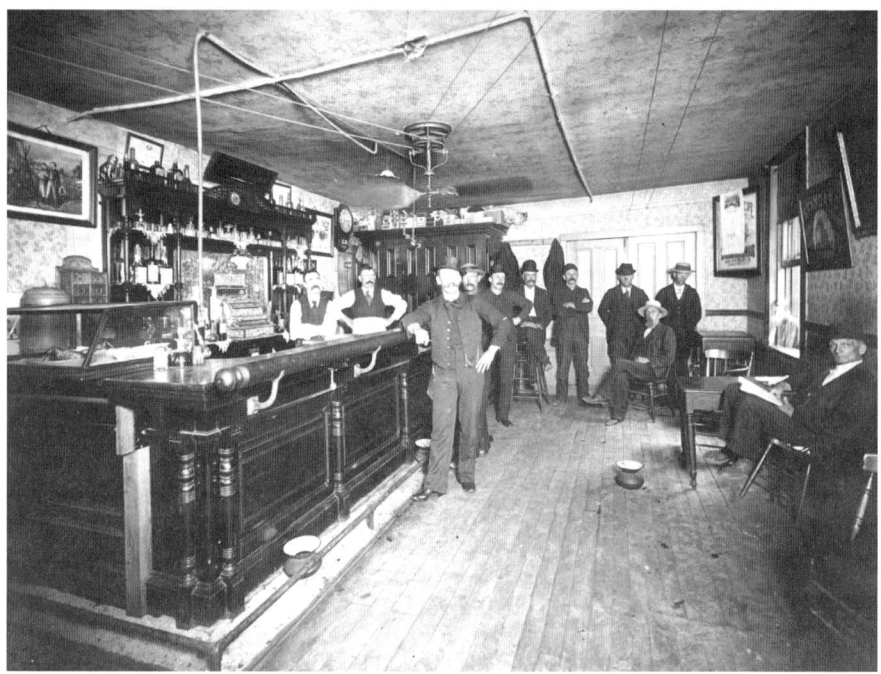

The interior of the Farmers' Tavern and Inn. Patrons would gather at midnight to witness the "noisy ghost." *Courtesy of Rochester Public Library.*

freedom, and perhaps lives, may point to one more element of the legend of Hoodoo Corner. It may be significant as well that the young eyewitness, Dixon, mentioned in his testimony that he had passed the corner at Main and Elm only moments before he heard the footsteps of Lyman and Barron.

In any case, despite the unanswered questions, the trial of Octavius Barron concluded. The closing argument for the prosecution lasted three hours, while the closing argument for the defense lasted four hours. The judge's instructions to the jury took another three hours. In the end, the thirty-nine jurors needed just fifty minutes for their deliberations. Their verdict: guilty!

## The Sentence

Once the jury had given its verdict, the only significant question that remained in the minds of many was Barron's sentence. There was some hope, or fear, depending on one's perspective, that a death sentence might be avoided because of Barron's age. But Judge Charles Wentworth quickly made clear, indicating at the very opening of his passing of sentence, that there would be no mercy from his court.

He said, speaking directly to Barron:

> *The evidence shows that you have long associated with the most vicious and depraved… That your companions were gamblers, blacklegs, and prostitutes, and that these habits and associations have prepared you for the commission of this last most fatal crime. Your heart is so effectively hardened that we dare not expect anything we may can reach or soften it. That can only be done by a power more than human.*
>
> *When you raised the weapon of death against Lyman, you doubtlessly supposed that no eye beheld your deed of blood, but the manner of this wonderful trial which has been made, shows that the All-seeing Eye was upon you, and saw your every movement. He has made it the occasion of showing His providence and His power. Before His tribunal you must be arraigned. The sentence of this court upon your case is that you be hung by the neck until you are dead.*
>
> *We must now add that the aggravated circumstances of your case forbid the hope of pardon or any mitigation of your punishment. You must now prepare for death. Your life has been worse than useless. We will hope that at least your death is of some profit to others, as a warning to deter them from a life of vice and crime.*

## The Confession

As preparations for carrying out the sentence got underway, the story of Octavius Barron took the kind of twist that one sometimes sees, or hopes to see, in a Hollywood movie. Although the legal proceedings were concluded, it is perhaps fair to say that issues of justice and redemption remained. And they would be addressed in Barron's final hours.

On the eve of his execution, Barron was allowed visitors. The first was his mother, Margaret, who, not content simply to say goodbye to her son, instead pleaded with him to confess, so that his soul would go to heaven. Observers claimed that Barron, at first, refused, still maintaining his innocence. But then, as his mother was leaving her son for the last time and "with a decency that he had never before displayed," Barron apologized to his mother, and admitted that he had murdered William Lyman. And what is more, that he wished to formally confess his deed. By this, as it turned out, he meant in both religious and legal terms.

The sheriff and two clergymen were summoned, one Roman Catholic and the other Protestant. Barron then gave a confession in the presence of these men, specifically to the Catholic priest, the Reverend Bernard O'Reilly of St. Patrick's Church. Barron reportedly confessed in full, clearing the names of the men who had been charged as his accomplices and accounting for the method by which he had secured and disposed of the murder weapon. Barron also said that he had thrown Lyman's still-missing satchel into the river. Finally, just hours before his death, Barron admitted to killing another man years before in a dispute over gambling. Barron allowed that his execution would be just punishment for that crime as well.

Barron then reportedly did his penance, praying in both French and Latin, and asked for God's forgiveness. When he was finished, Barron turned to the sheriff and asked for one thing in return for the confession. He requested that upon his stepping onto the gallows, he "be hanged right away."

This seems at first glance an odd request. But the likely reasoning for the request lies in the nature of execution by hanging. It is arguably one of the most brutal methods for carrying out a death sentence. There are many variables for an executioner to consider when conducting an execution by hanging, such as the height and weight of the man, the length of the drop and the precise placement of the rope around the neck. These factors are crucial in determining the length of time it takes a man to die and the amount of pain he will suffer in the process.

# The Murder of William Lyman

The complications of death by hanging were common knowledge in nineteenth-century America, as the method was widely used. The results were sometimes quite gruesome, depending on the skill, attention to detail and conscientiousness of the executioner. In fact, the highly variable outcomes of death by hanging are the main reason it became gradually outlawed as a method of capital punishment in the United States during the twentieth century.

It seems that Barron was aware of these possibilities and was essentially making a request for the most humane death possible. In this period, the two most commonly used methods of hanging were known as the short drop and long drop. The short drop was the condemned man's worst fear. Commonly used prior to 1850, it usually involved a cart, horse or stool, upon which the condemned was stood. Once the noose was around his neck, the support was removed. The resulting drop could be as little as a few inches, which meant that the prisoner slowly strangled to death. The weight of his body and his struggle worked to tighten the noose, which would eventually close off his airway and/or the carotid arteries, which supply blood to the brain. Not only could this be an excruciatingly slow death—strangulation often took ten to twenty minutes—it was often quite painful.

The long drop was developed as a more humane way to execute death sentences and came into widespread use in the latter nineteenth century. Unlike the short drop, in which everyone fell roughly the same distance, in this method the person's body weight determined the distance of the drop, usually between six and eight

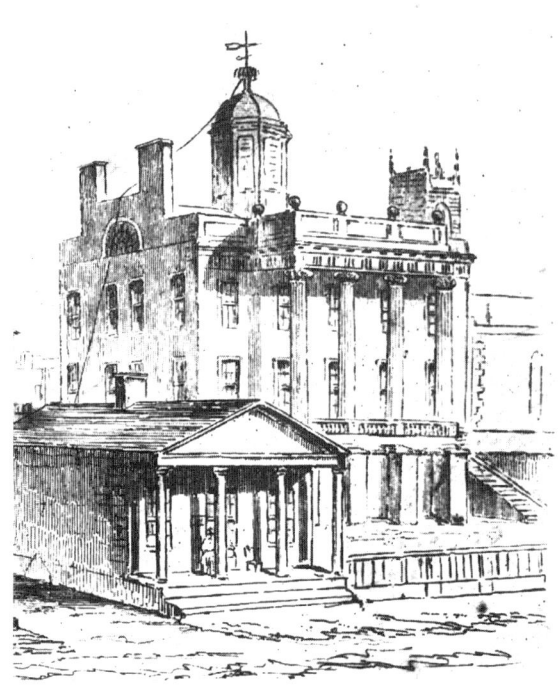

An illustration of Rochester's first courthouse. Ironically, this is where Octavius Barron would be found guilty of murder and sentenced to hang. *Courtesy of Rochester Public Library.*

feet. The method was also the best way to ensure that the individual's neck would be broken, resulting in instant death. There were, however, sometimes complications with this method as well, particularly unintended decapitations. Nevertheless, the odds of a faster, less painful death were better with this method of hanging.

When Barron asked to be hanged "right away" in return for his confession, he was, in effect, asking that the long drop be employed and perhaps that the executioner be carefully chosen as well. Barron was hoping for an executioner who would do his best to ensure that he not suffer needlessly.

## The Execution

Given the overwhelming interest in the trial and the anger and outrage of Rochester's citizens over the crime and its perpetrator, it is not surprising that many residents were hoping for a public execution. But the Act against Public Executions, passed by the legislature of New York only three years previously, meant that they would not get their wish. Instead, the execution would be held indoors on July 25, 1838, between the hours of one and two o'clock, on the first floor of the Monroe County Jail. There were forty-nine witnesses in attendance, including many public officials, physicians, judges, prison officers and noble citizens of Rochester.

According to a newspaper account at the time, "Barron appeared on the first floor of the jail at 1:40 pm, accompanied by the Sheriff and the two clergymen who were praying in Latin and in French. Barron wore a white roundabout, white pantaloons, and a ruffle shirt. His countenance betook great horror." But, witnesses agreed, "Barron stepped up onto the platform of his own accord and stood without trembling. He asked for the forgiveness of those he had injured, and also for the forgiveness of God."

The noose was placed around his neck, and the supporting platform was removed. "He died with little struggle, holding a Catholic cross in his right hand." This ended the ignominious life of Octavius Barron.

## Postscript

William's widow, Amanda, moved back to her hometown of Hadley, Massachusetts. Fifteen years later, she married Cyrus White, a distant cousin of hers. In the census of 1880, Amanda was reported to be still living in

# The Murder of William Lyman

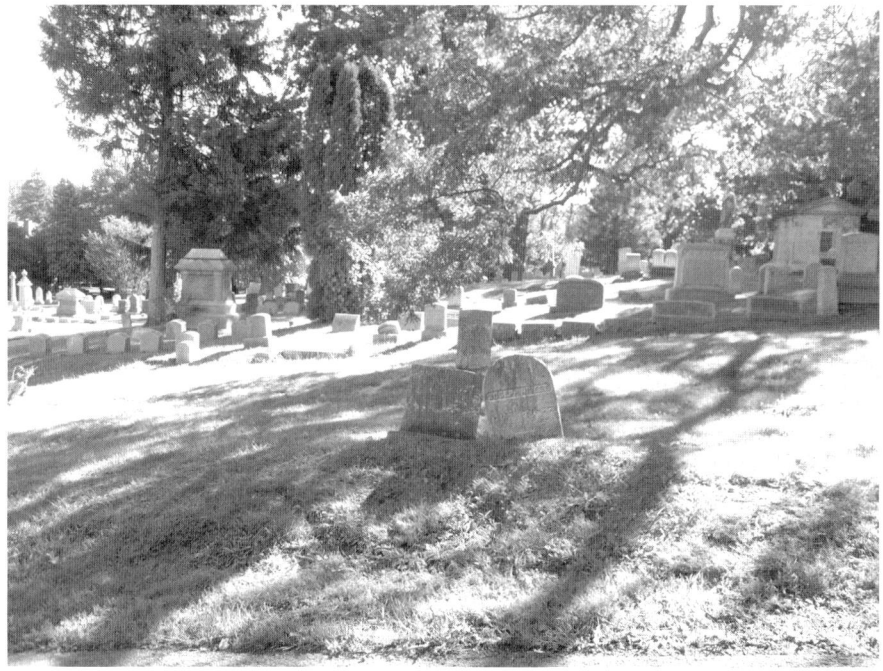

The grave sites of William Lyman and Octavius Barron, who are both interred in Mount Hope Cemetery in section D. *Courtesy of the author.*

Hadley with her eldest son, William. She was then eighty-three. She never returned to Rochester.

Octavius Barron was buried in the public grounds of Mount Hope cemetery, which was newly established during the summer of 1838. Barron's life was a bizarre series of improbable firsts: Rochester's first murderer and first person executed in the city, probably the first person ever hanged using the long-drop method and the first person interred in the newly established cemetery. Today, Octavius Barron lies in an unmarked grave.

As the case of William Lyman and Octavius Barron demonstrates, the issue of civil rights was to become prominent in American life. It was not an accident of history that the two opposing attorneys were both significantly involved in the Underground Railroad. The first antislavery speech ever given in the United States was delivered in Rochester. As we now turn to tales of hoodoo doctors, radical abolitionists and the Underground Railroad, we delve further into the origins of Hoodoo Corner.

# CHAPTER 9
# Hoodoo Doctor

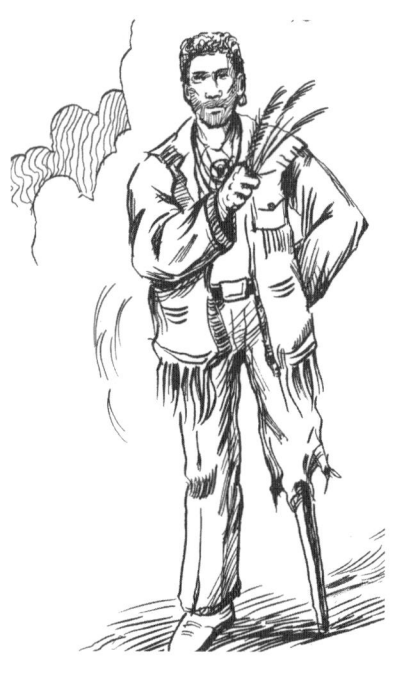

The word hoodoo is, of course, the best indication of how it came to be connected to a corner in Rochester, though the etymology, as noted earlier, points to more than one simple meaning. In this chapter, we take up the final, and perhaps most intriguing, element of the mix of associations and events that created the legend: black culture and Rochester's prominence in the abolitionist movement of the early to mid-nineteenth century.

Definitive data on the black population of the Rochester area is hard to come by, but the first African American who appears in the historical record is Asa Dunbar, a mulatto who opened a clearing on Irondequoit Bay in 1795, which later became the northeast corner of the city. Austin Steward, who arrived in 1816, was probably the first black businessman in Rochester. He opened a meat market shortly after his arrival and did fairly well for a number of years until he left to help establish the free-black colony at Wilberforce, Ontario. In 1823, the African Methodist Episcopal Zion Society—only the third church established in Rochester—

was founded. By 1840, Rochester's total population was approximately twenty thousand, of which just over four hundred were blacks. Most were laborers, but there were skilled tradesmen, clergy and merchants as well.[33]

Many of these black residents brought with them a set of folk practices called hoodoo. It appears at first glance—as it seemed even to early lexicographers—that the word hoodoo must be a variation on the term "voodoo." But this is, in fact, not the case. Though they sound similar to our ear, the terms are derived from different African languages. The best current evidence suggests that the word hoodoo was brought over with African slaves who spoke a language called Hausa. In Hausa, the word *hu'du'ba* is a verb, and it means "to arouse resentment, produce retribution." As the word evolved, it came to describe a system of folkloric practices some might call magic. And, as suggested by the root, the magic practices are employed against one's enemies.

Hoodoo is thus quite distinct from the English word voodoo, which came into the lexicon via the Louisiana Creole "voudou." The original term came from slaves who spoke a language called Ewe, and it is originally a noun that refers to a specific African deity.[34] While both are West African languages, they are spoken by different ethnic groups. Perhaps the best evidence for its dissimilarity is that the Hausa and Ewe come from different language families; Ewe is a tonal language, while Hausa is not.

The dissimilarities are obvious in practice as well. Hoodoo does not have a deity, hierarchy, theology, laity or liturgical practice. It is a body of folk practices and beliefs, rather than a proper religion, as voodoo is. Voodoo has a priestly caste and its own cosmology. These very differences help explain the persistence and resiliency of hoodoo, as it was carried far and wide, easily adapting to its environment. While there are leaders of a sort—hoodoo doctors—the body of knowledge and practice is open to any member of the community. Many of the practices—homemade potions and charms, candles, magnetic lodestones, animal bones and "mojo" bags containing mixtures of herbs, minerals and roots—are known and used by average members of these communities, through enculturation rather than structured teaching. The knowledge is simply passed from one person to another.

Many anthropologists and folklorists, like Zora Neale Hurston, became interested in hoodoo in the late nineteenth century and systematically collected knowledge about it. Their findings suggest that hoodoo is highly syncretistic by easily integrating Christian cosmology and theology within the body of existing practices. Christianity found fertile soil among slaves, though it did not necessarily displace acculturated beliefs like hoodoo. There seems to be quite a comfortable fit between the two, in fact, perhaps because hoodoo is characteristically described as possessing an Old Testament component. That is to say, there is a strong notion of good and evil, and God plays an active role in exacting retribution. As one black man explained: "[In] Hoodooism, anythin' da' chew do is de plan of God. Undastan', God have somepin to do wit' evah' thin' you do, if it's good or bad. He's got somepin to do wit' it. Jis what's fo' you, you'll git it."[35] In other words, a hoodoo "spell" does not work on its own. The question of the outcome is in God's hands; the individual who uses hoodoo is essentially helping the divine along, taking concrete, if magical, steps to achieve the desired outcome.

In this sense, though the particular thing that an individual is seeking might be bad—in that it may affect another person negatively—in order for it to happen, it must be God's will and, most importantly, serve the cause of justice in a larger sense. In the antebellum south, in particular, this was a powerful notion, a kind of belief in karma, if also a goosing of its workings. Such a powerful and subversive notion might be seen as a threat to the established order. In many plantation areas, slaves organized underground churches, giving rise to an "invisible church" where slaves mixed Christianity with African beliefs. These underground churches provided psychological refuge from the white world and were a place where the admixture of religion could not be controlled by whites.

This mix of the two traditions horrified many devout Christians who came into contact with it and who believed it to be blasphemy. Nora Neale Hurston notes the unorthodoxy of the admixture: "The way we tell it, hoodoo started way back there before everything. Six days of magic spells and mighty words and the world with its elements above and below was made."[36] In this way, biblical figures—including, most notably and frequently, Moses—were recast as hoodoo doctors. And the Bible became a source of spells (especially the Book of Psalms) and sometimes a talisman as well. Some of the antipathy to hoodoo from white culture undoubtedly came from this syncretistic approach; many would have viewed this as a sacrilege, a perversion of Christianity. It would only have added to tension and suspicion in a place where any uncontrolled gathering of blacks was feared.

\*\*\*

# Hoodoo Doctor

Although it is clear that the word was used in the English vernacular much earlier, one of the earliest written uses of the word hoodoo is an 1891 journal entry by Samuel C. Taylor. Taylor happened to be on a train near Birmingham, Alabama, during the Civil War in 1862 when a black man boarded. Taylor was so intrigued by the man he would learn was a hoodoo doctor that he drew a sketch of him and devoted four pages of his journal to a description of him as well.

Taylor wrote:

> *He was an odd-looking creature. He looked to be about 40 years old and near I should say about 180 pounds, stocky and hearty. Stood 5'8". He had a fine-shaped head and a very intelligent face and bright eyes; his head was shaved close to the scalp except in front, where there was left a bunch as large as my fist. His right leg was off just below the knee, was finished with a wooden leg. He was quick in his movement, and appeared to be well-known, judging by the number that spoke to him when he entered the car and seated himself directly opposite of where I was setting. He had three coats on, they were just made of patches of cloth of various colors and kinds…[and] around his neck and body was a length of chains, small and large, and reaching to his waist; some kind of brass, others of silver plate, and the larger ones of iron.….He was a very good talker and did much talking.*

Taylor further relates that when the man completed his journey, getting off the train after only four miles or so, a "colored porter" approached and apologized for the man's behavior. Taylor had not been offended, however, and was so intrigued by him that he questioned the porter about him. Taylor was told that the man

> *is a hoodoo doctor. He has been on his regular monthly trip among the Negroes in this valley. They look upon him as infallible, and what he says is law. A Negro feels sick, the doctor calls. He asks no questions but taking a brass ring out of his pocket, holds it in his fingers, mutters a few hoodoo words. When he gives it to the patient with a vial of his medicine and goes away, the chap is satisfied that he is alright and nine times out of ten, he gets well.* [The porter said:] *"You saw him in rags but when he gets to his station; he takes those off and gets into a decent suit. He is educated and can be gentlemanly if he wants to be, he has studied medicine and is by far the most influential man among his color in this part of the state. And he has plenty of money."*[37]

It is clear that the man Taylor encountered that day is what has also been called a "root doctor," a relatively common figure in black communities of the old south. Traditionally, a root doctor was a nomad who traveled from town to town peddling his services, although many did not travel but rather worked as community advisors of a sort. In fact, one of the earliest references to a root doctor comes in *Narrative of the Life of Frederick Douglass, an American Slave*, which was originally published in 1845.

## Frederick Douglass

Frederick Douglass (circa 1817–1895) was born a slave in Talbot County, Maryland. When he was sixteen years old, having already acquired a reputation for difficulty, he was loaned out to a neighboring farmer, Edward Covey. Covey had a reputation as a slave breaker, and Douglass was regularly whipped by him. After a particularly difficult period, fearing that he would be whipped to death, Douglass ran away. He found temporary refuge with another slave family in the area but was advised to return to Covey's farm, as he was imperiling the family as well as himself. Douglass took the advice, and decided to return.

He later wrote:

> *I started off to Covey's in the morning, (Saturday morning,) wearied in body and broken in spirit. I got no supper that night, or breakfast that morning. I reached Covey's about nine o'clock; and just as I was getting over the fence that divided Mrs. Kemp's fields from ours, out ran Covey with his cowskin, to give me another whipping. Before he could reach me, I succeeded in getting to the cornfield; and as the corn was very high, it afforded me the means of hiding. He seemed very angry, and searched for me a long time. My behavior was altogether unaccountable. He finally gave up the chase, thinking, I suppose, that as I must come home for something to eat; he would give himself no further trouble in looking for me. I spent that day mostly in the woods, having the alternative before me to go home and be whipped to death, or stay in the woods and be starved to death.*
>
> *That night, I fell in with Sandy Jenkins, a slave with whom I was somewhat acquainted. Sandy had a free wife, who lived about four miles from Mr. Covey's; and it being Saturday, he was on his way to see her. I told him my circumstances, and he very kindly invited me to go home with him. I went home with him, and talked this whole matter over…I found Sandy*

# Hoodoo Doctor

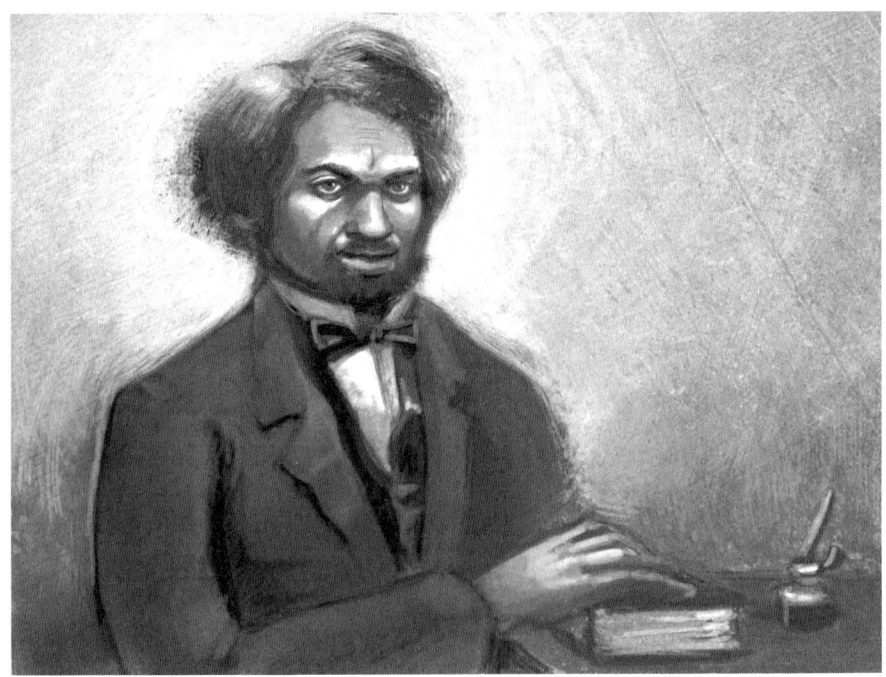

An illustration of Frederick Douglass, 1818–1895. He was a former slave and Rochester newspaper publisher. His autobiography contains the first written mention of a hoodoo doctor.

*an old adviser* [sic]. *He told me, with great solemnity, I must go back to Covey; but that before I went, I must go with him into another part of the woods, where there was a certain root, which, if I would take some of it with me, carrying it always on my right side, would render it impossible for Mr. Covey, or any other white man, to whip me. He said he had carried it for years; and since he had done so, he had never received a blow, and never expected to, while he carried it. I at first rejected the idea, that the simple carrying of a root in my pocket would have any such effect as he had said, and was not disposed to take it; but Sandy impressed the necessity with much earnestness… To please him, I at length took the root, and, according to his direction, carried it upon my right side.*

*All went well till Monday morning. On this morning, the virtue of the root was fully tested. Long before daylight, I was called to go and rub, curry, and feed the horses. I obeyed, and was glad to obey. But whilst thus engaged, whilst in the act of throwing down some blades from the loft, Mr. Covey entered the stable with a long rope; and just as I was half out of the loft, he caught hold of my legs, and was about tying me. As soon as I found what he was up to, I gave a sudden spring, and as I did so, he holding to my legs, I was brought sprawling on the stable floor. Mr. Covey seemed now to think he had me, and could do what he pleased; but at this moment from whence came the spirit I don't know I resolved to fight; and suiting my action to the resolution, I seized Covey hard by the throat; and as I did so, I rose. He held on to me, and I to him. My resistance was so entirely unexpected, that Covey seemed taken all aback. He trembled like a leaf.*

*This gave me assurance, and I held him uneasy, causing the blood to run where I touched him with the ends of my fingers. Mr. Covey soon called out to Hughes for help. Hughes came, and, while Covey held me, attempted to tie my right hand. While he was in the act of doing so, I watched my chance, and gave him a heavy kick close under the ribs. This kick fairly sickened Hughes, so that he left me in the hands of Mr. Covey. This kick had the effect of not only weakening Hughes, but Covey also. When he saw Hughes bending over with pain, his courage quailed. He asked me if I meant to persist in my resistance. I told him I did, come what might; that he had used me like a brute for six months, and that I was determined to be used so no longer.*

*With that, he strove to drag me to a stick that was lying just out of the stable door. He meant to knock me down. But just as he was leaning over to get the stick, I seized him with both hands by his collar, and brought him by a sudden snatch to the ground…We were at it for nearly two hours. Covey at length let me go, puffing and blowing at a great rate, saying that if I had not resisted, he would not have whipped me half so much. The truth was that he had not whipped me at all. I considered him as getting entirely the worst end of the bargain; for he had drawn no blood from me, but I had from him.*

*The whole six months afterwards that I spent with Mr. Covey, he never laid the weight of his finger upon me in anger. He would occasionally say he didn't want to get hold of me again. "No," thought I, "you need not; for you will come off worse than you did before."*

*This battle with Mr. Covey was the turning-point in my career as a slave. It rekindled the few expiring embers of freedom, and revived within me a sense of my own manhood…I felt as I never felt before. It was a glorious resurrection from the tomb of slavery to the heaven of freedom. My long-crushed spirit rose, cowardice departed, bold defiance took its place; and I now resolved that, however long I might remain a slave in form, the day had passed forever when I could be a slave in fact. I did not hesitate to let it be known of me, that the white man who expected to succeed in whipping, must also succeed in killing me. From this time I was never again what might be called fairly whipped, though I remained a slave four years afterwards. I had several fights, but was never whipped.*[38]

This passage beautifully illustrates the central idea of hoodoo, that it is a way for a man to avail himself of energies in the environment, a way of accessing supernatural forces to improve the circumstances of his daily life by gaining practical power. Hoodoo means bringing luck and throwing curses—manipulating the actions of elemental forces through throwing tricks or spells—nearly always in the service of protecting oneself. As Henry Hyatt, perhaps the single most dedicated student of the topic, wrote, "To catch a spirit or to protect your spirit against the catching, or to release your caught spirit: This is the complete theory and practice of hoodoo."[39]

While most hoodoo doctors, like the one Douglass met, were black, there were also white and Native American practitioners. There is certainly a resonance in hoodoo with much of Indian spiritual practice, particularly in the idea of contact with ancestors or other spirits of the dead. The forming of communities between Indians and runaway slaves in areas beyond the "frontier" (as it moved westward) is well documented. This raises interesting questions about the connection between hoodoo and "outsider" cultures and whether, in this case, the legend of Hoodoo Corner grew from a particular meeting of black and Indian cultures or a perception of that meeting, at any rate.

There is clear evidence of the Indian origin of the site, where two key trails once crossed, with a burial ground nearby. We can only speculate, however, as to whether there were any Native American practitioners of hoodoo in the Rochester area, though it's arguable that Handsome Lake might qualify, particularly for white settlers, who might not have made crucial distinctions between what would today be called alternate belief systems. It seems likely that the legend grew up over time, in recognition of the outsiders who frequented the area and the odd and eerie series of events occurring there. Clearly, however, there was a sense that mysterious things happened at this site, and at some point, the word "hoodoo" became attached to it, perhaps as late as the mid-nineteenth century, when, as the rest of Douglass's story shows, blacks became a more visible and controversial part of Rochester.

✳ ✳ ✳

Douglass is, of course, a towering figure in African American history, and he lived in Rochester during a pivotal period, when it was a center not only of abolitionism but of many key movements of the mid-nineteenth century. In the broadest sense, Douglass was responsible for bringing the realities of slavery to the attention of white Americans and, perhaps more importantly, disproving in the way that he did so that claims of the inherent intellectual superiority of whites were false. In his long life, he was a slave, abolitionist, women's suffragist, editor, orator, lecturer, writer and statesman.

Born in a shack on the eastern shore of Maryland, he was separated from his mother, Harriet Bailey, when he was still an infant. She died when he was about seven, and Douglass lived with his maternal grandmother, Betty Bailey. The identity of his father is unknown. Early in his life, Douglass claimed that he was told his father was a white man, perhaps his mother's owner, Aaron Anthony. Later, he said he knew nothing of his father's identity. Douglass was eventually separated from his grandmother and moved to the Wye House plantation, where Anthony worked as overseer. When Anthony died, Douglass was given to Lucretia Auld, the wife of Thomas Auld. She promptly sent Douglass to work for Thomas's brother, Hugh, in Baltimore. It would be a critical turning point for Douglass.

When he was about twelve, Hugh Auld's wife, Sophia, taught him the alphabet. In doing this, she was breaking the law against teaching slaves to read, and when her husband found out, he suggested that she stop, saying that if a slave learned to read, he would become dissatisfied with his condition. She complied with her husband's wishes, but Douglass took note of the man's fears and determined to learn to read. He seized opportunities that came his way, paying close attention to white children doing their lessons and to the white men around him who used writing in their work. Douglass taught himself so well that when he was eventually hired out to William Freeland, he taught other slaves on the plantation how to read, using the New Testament as a primer in Sunday school sessions. His tutorials proceeded quietly for about six weeks, but as word spread, interest among the slaves grew, and eventually more than forty began attending the Sunday school literacy sessions. While Freeland was unperturbed, nearby plantation owners became angry and burst in on the group one Sunday, dispersing it with clubs and stones.

This helped to cement Douglass's reputation as a problem slave. He made his first escape attempt while living at Freeland's. After the Sunday school was broken up, Douglass was sent back to Thomas Auld's, but Auld was dissatisfied with him as well, so he sent him to Covey's, where Douglass made another failed escape attempt. In 1837, Douglass fell in love with Anna Murray, a free black woman who lived in Baltimore. This seems to have provided just the motivation and contacts he needed to free himself. On September 3, 1838, Douglass successfully escaped by boarding a train to Havre de Grace, Maryland. He dressed in a sailor's uniform and carried identification papers provided by a free black seaman. Douglass crossed the Susquehanna River by ferry and then continued by train to Wilmington, Delaware. From there, he went by steamboat to Philadelphia and then to New York. The entire journey took less than twenty-four hours. Shortly thereafter, Douglass married Anna, with whom he would have five children.

From New York, Douglass wrote to a friend: "I felt as one might feel upon escape from a den of hungry lions." He settled for a time in New Bedford, Massachusetts, and threw himself into activity, joining a black church and attending abolitionist meetings. He subscribed to William Lloyd Garrison's weekly abolitionist paper, the *Liberator*, and in 1841, he heard Garrison speak at a meeting of the Bristol Anti-Slavery Society. Shortly thereafter, Douglass delivered his first speech at the Massachusetts Anti-Slavery Society's annual convention in Nantucket. In 1843, Douglass participated in the American Anti-Slavery Society's Hundred Conventions project, a six-month tour of meeting halls throughout the eastern and midwestern United States and began writing his memoir, *Narrative of the Life of Frederick Douglass, an American Slave*.

Its publication in 1845 opened a new chapter in his life. Some skeptics attacked the book, arguing that a black man could not have produced it. Nevertheless, the book received generally positive reviews, and it became an immediate bestseller. But this was also problematic: many feared that the publicity would draw the attention of Douglass's legal owner, Hugh Auld, who might attempt to get his "property" back. Douglass therefore left the United States in August 1845 and spent the next two years touring and lecturing in Great Britain. It was during this trip that Douglass became officially free. A group of British supporters raised the money to buy Douglass's freedom from Auld.

Thus, when Douglass returned to the United States in 1847, it was as a free man. He and Anna bought a home in Rochester. Douglass opened the next chapter of his life in December of that year, when the first issue of his new weekly, the *North Star*, rolled off the press. The paper was headquartered in the basement of the African Methodist Episcopal Zion Church, in which Douglass would become an ordained minister. Effusive praise and support followed publication, though not all Rochester citizens were pleased to see

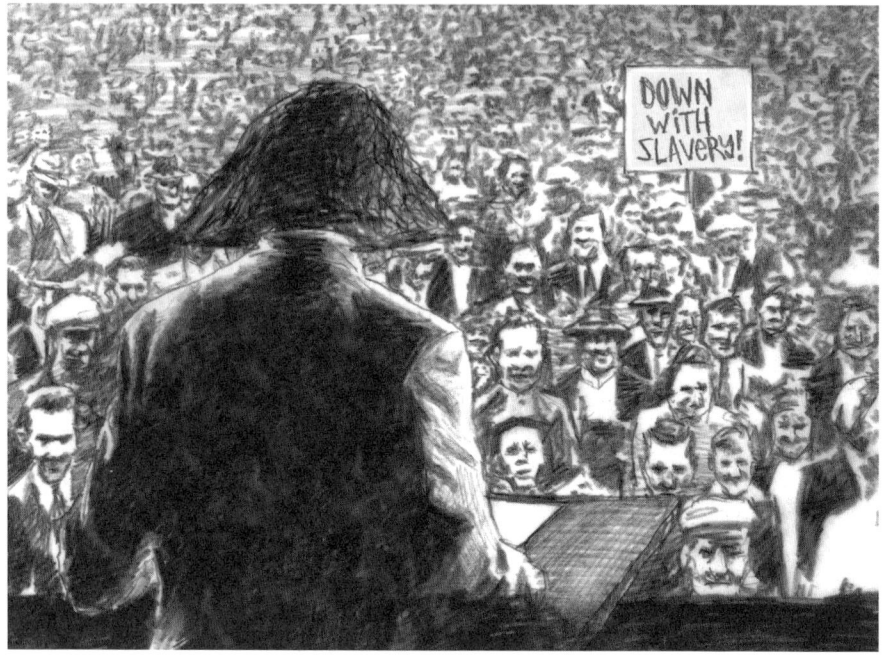

An illustration of Frederick Douglass speaking before an abolitionist rally. The first major antislavery speech ever given was in Rochester.

another antislavery paper, especially one edited by a black man. The *New York Herald*, for instance, urged the citizens of Rochester to dump Douglass's printing press into Lake Ontario.

It is no coincidence that the masthead of the *North Star* read: "Right is of no sex. Truth is of no color. God is the Father of us all, and we are all Brethren." With the establishment of this newspaper, Rochester became a national center of the antislavery movement, as it was becoming a national center of the suffragist movement. Susan B. Anthony, also a citizen of Rochester, was a close friend of Douglass's. He was one of the few men who attended the 1848 National Women's Rights Convention that was held at nearby Seneca Falls. Douglass gave an eloquent speech, noting he could not accept the right to vote himself as a black man if a woman could not also claim that right. He clearly saw the issue of women's rights as fundamentally the same as slavery; it was an inherent discounting of the abilities of a person. He said, "In this denial of the right to participate in government, not merely the degradation of woman and the perpetuation of a great injustice happen, but the maiming and repudiation of one-half of the moral and intellectual power of the government of the world." Douglass was a firm believer in the equality of all people, whether black, female, Native American or recent immigrant. He said, "I would unite with anybody to do right and with nobody to do wrong."

The women's rights and antislavery movements were entwined in many ways. Both became entwined as well with the emerging spiritualist movement, which will be further discussed in the next chapter. Many people were active in multiple causes, including other Rochester residents like Lucretia Mott and Elizabeth Cady Stanton, both of whom were lifelong friends of Douglass. But this did not necessarily make things easier for him. The suffragists, in particular, drew much hostile press; for instance, the thirty-five women and thirty-two men who went to Seneca Falls were described as "man-haters" and "hermaphrodites." The hostility of the press and the public also sometimes extended into Douglass's private life.

Douglass and his wife, Anna, had, by most accounts, a solid marriage. But Douglass also admired the educated, politically active women with whom he spent so much time working. Douglass was an extraordinarily busy, active figure. When he was forced, for instance, to return to the lecture circuit to raise money for the newspaper during its first year, he was on the road for six months. In the spring of 1848, he had to mortgage his home to fund the paper. And the demands on his time grew, as did his stature and national reputation. While he roamed far and wide, his wife remained at home, raising their family, remaining uneducated, nonpolitical, and disengaged. Douglass went so far as to hire a teacher for her one year, hoping to bridge the intellectual gap between them. But the effort failed, and Anna remained almost totally illiterate.

At any rate, although there was much goodwill and support among the population of Rochester, and particularly the abolitionist and women's right groups and the printer's union, Douglass had financial difficulty with the newspaper. Production costs were high, and subscriptions grew slowly, particularly among blacks. Some 80 percent of subscribers were white, which might have reflected the economic realities of the black population.

Scandal erupted in 1848, when Julia Griffiths, a friend from England, arrived to help Douglass with his financial problems. She had raised money to help launch the paper, and now she was prepared to fight for its survival. She set herself to putting the *North Star*'s finances in order, and Douglass was eventually able to regain possession of his home. In addition to becoming Douglass's office and business manager, Griffiths soon became his almost-constant companion. She arranged his lectures, dealt with the paper's finances and accompanied him to meetings.

Most people in Rochester adjusted to the sight of the black leader and the white woman walking arm-in-arm down the street. Nevertheless, rumors began to fly, not least because Griffiths lived in the same house with Douglass and his wife. Anna was reportedly uneasy about the rumors and idle gossip. Newspapers picked up the controversy, and Douglass was attacked, by the Garrisonians, in particular, for involving the abolitionist movement in a scandal. In 1852, Griffiths spared Douglass further embarrassment by moving out of his home. She remained his close associate until 1855, when she returned to England.

In 1850, Douglass became involved with the Underground Railroad, the system set up by antislavery groups to bring runaway slaves to free states in the north or Canada. Given Rochester's proximity to the Canadian border, and the number of its residents who were sympathetic to abolitionist causes, it's not surprising that Rochester became a key hub in the system. Many of those who were crucial to functioning in the area were Quakers (Susan B. Anthony, Lucretia Mott and Isaac and Amy Post, for example), though the issue led to divisions in the sect as well. It was illegal to aid a runaway slave, and some Quakers believed that breaking U.S. law was wrong; others, however, believed that answering "no" to the question of whether they were hiding slaves was not lying, because no human being could by rights own another, and therefore there was no such thing as a slave.

Douglass worked closely with William C. Bloss, a Methodist. Born in 1795 in Massachusetts, Bloss had arrived at abolitionism through a series of events that practically traced the history of Rochester. In 1823, he built a tavern on the Erie Canal, but a few years later, he became a temperance advocate and dumped the contents of his tavern into it. He sold the building and moved into Rochester in 1830. He was a supporter of the anti-Masonic movement and later became involved in the antislavery movement. He worked with Thomas James, an African American minister, to organize a local antislavery society. According to James, the first of three meetings scheduled for this purpose was held in the courthouse and attracted a large crowd of the curious. At the second meeting, onlookers asked numerous questions, and at "the third they drowned with their noise the voices of the speakers and… turned out the lights." At this point, Bloss, whom James describes as "not a man to be cowed by opposition," got a meeting room for the group in the Third Presbyterian Church, near Hoodoo Corner. There, under the protection of locked doors, the harassed advocates organized the society.

Bloss's home on East Avenue, just across the street from Hoodoo Corner, was a stop on the Underground Railroad, as was Douglass's own home.

## Hoodoo Doctor

He sometimes hosted nearly a dozen runaway slaves at a time. Eventually, Douglass became the superintendent of the system in his area. He often found runaways sitting on the steps of his newspaper office when he arrived for work in the morning. Over the years, he and Anna sheltered hundreds of these men and women.

As the national political discussion over slavery grew more heated in the 1850s, so did Douglass's relationships with some in the abolitionist movement. For Douglass, starting the *North Star* marked the end of his dependence on Garrison and other white abolitionists. The newspaper meant that Douglass was covering problems facing blacks around the country, not just the enslaved in the south. Douglass had heated arguments with many white abolitionists and with fellow black activists

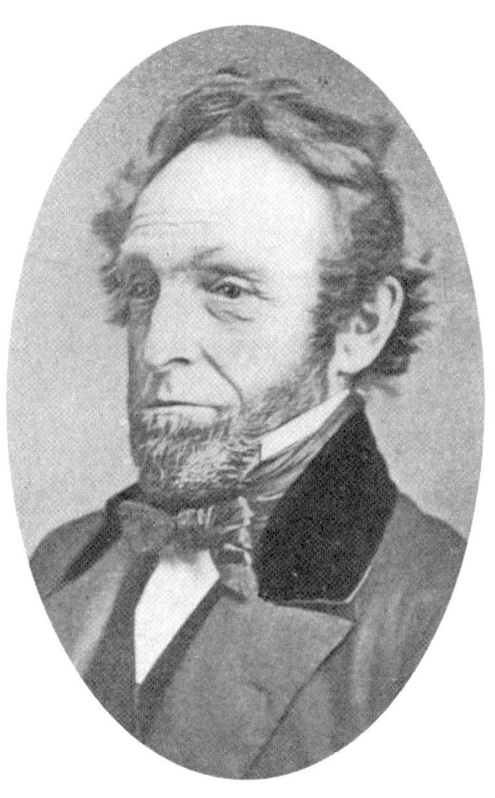

William C. Bloss, 1795–1863, abolitionist and temperance leader. His home, located near Main and Elm Streets, was used to shelter runaway slaves. *Courtesy of Rochester Museum & Science Center.*

over these issues, the beginnings of dialogue within the African American community over its own destiny. And, as the country headed toward civil war, political rhetoric in all quarters tended to grow more inflamed.

Over time, tensions between Douglass and Garrison mounted, particularly because Douglass's views on the best tactics to end slavery were changing and differed markedly from Garrison's. Douglass began to question Garrison's insistence on nonviolence and passive resistance, though there was an apparently opposite contradiction between them as well: Douglass believed that the founding documents of the United States (the Declaration of Independence and the U.S. Constitution) provided a path out of slavery, while Garrison believed the Constitution was irredeemable.

In any event, in 1847, Douglass met with the militant white abolitionist John Brown. At abolitionist meetings, Douglass began telling his audiences that he would be pleased to hear that the slaves in the south had revolted. The final split between Douglass and Garrison took place in June 1851 at the annual meeting of the American Anti-Slavery Society. Douglass shocked his associates by publicly announcing that he intended to urge the readers of the *North Star* to engage in active politics, which suggested the possibility of violent resistance. Garrison and his allies launched a vicious assault against him during the following months.

But Douglass had no intention of reversing course. In a speech given in Rochester on Independence Day in 1852, Douglass said:

> *What to the American slave is your Fourth of July? I answer a day that reveals to him more than all other days of the year, the gross injustice and cruelty to which he is the constant victim. To him your celebration is a sham; your boasted liberty an unholy license; your national greatness, swelling vanity; your sounds of rejoicing are empty and heartless; your shouts of liberty and equality, hollow mock; your prayers and hymns, your sermons and thanksgivings, with all your religious parade and solemnity, are to him mere bombast, fraud, deception, impiety, and hypocrisy—a thin veil to cover up crimes which would disgrace a nation of savages. There is not a nation of the earth guilty of practices more shocking and bloody than are the people of these United States at this very hour.*[40]

Douglass actively engaged in politics in his own town as well. Rochester's public schools would not admit black students, and Douglass initially enrolled his oldest child, Rosetta, in a private school. Even there, Rosetta was segregated from white students, however, so Douglass hired a woman to teach his children at home. But as his children grew older, he became more and more dissatisfied with the situation. He began a campaign to end segregation in Rochester's school system, and in 1857, his efforts succeeded. In the spring of 1859, John Brown traveled to Rochester to appeal to Douglass one final time to formally join his movement, but again Douglass declined.

The stakes, however, were raised in October 1859, when John Brown and his men seized the U.S. Armory at Harpers Ferry. The next night, federal troops led by Colonel Robert E. Lee stormed the building, capturing Brown and killing approximately half of the band of twenty-two or so men, including two of Brown's sons. The events, which recalled Nat Turner's

Rebellion of 1841, were deeply shocking and frightening in the south, as it seemed to mark a new phase in the abolitionist movement.[41] Douglass was lecturing in Philadelphia when he heard about the events at the armory, and he was warned that letters had been found that implicated him in the attack. In fact, some newspaper headlines about the event contained Douglass's name.

Douglass, aware that he stood no chance of a fair trial if he were captured, fled to Canada. While in Canada, Douglass wrote letters in his own defense, explaining his flight and that he had refused to help Brown. One of the men captured during the raid said that Douglass had promised to appear at Harpers Ferry with reinforcements. Douglass denied this accusation, saying that he would never approve of attacks on federal property. But though he could not condone the raid, he praised Brown as a "noble old hero."

In November 1859, Douglass sailed to England to begin a lecture tour, a trip he had planned long before the incident at Harpers Ferry. The news of his near arrest increased his audiences, and his lectures stirred up more sympathy for the antislavery cause. In May 1860, as he was about to continue his lecture tour in France, word reached him that his youngest child, Annie, had died. Heartbroken, Douglass returned home, going through Canada to avoid detection.

By the time of the Civil War, Douglass was one of the most famous black men in the country. He continued his work as a writer, thinker and lecturer during the war. He left Rochester in 1872, after his house burned down, probably as the result of arson. He moved to Washington, D.C., started another newspaper and became deeply involved in post-Emancipation causes. Douglass's wife died in 1882. Two years later, he married Helen Pitts, a feminist. The couple faced a storm of controversy, as she was both white and nearly twenty years his junior. On February 20, 1895, Douglass attended a meeting of the National Council of Women. Shortly after he returned home that evening, he suffered an apparent heart attack or stroke and died. He is buried in Mount Hope Cemetery in Rochester, not far from the gravesite of Octavius Barron.

As the story of Douglass shows, the practice of root traditions was deeply important in American black culture of the nineteenth century. With its intimations of dark supernatural forces, and as these practices were often used by blacks to defend themselves psychologically and spiritually from the pressures of their daily lives in a slave-owning society, hoodoo was feared and disdained by many in the dominant culture. It is easy to see how the term came to be used in a pejorative sense, signifying a negative view of

African American spiritual practices, with more than a dollop of fear as well. Thus the word sometimes contained the same jeering quality that the term voodoo does.

This is also because the kind of people who practiced hoodoo, like Douglass, were also political activists and tended to go outside the bounds of what might be considered polite society. Many abolitionists, notably the Quakers, were committed enough to their beliefs to break the law, for instance, to provide aid and refuge for runaway slaves. And many of these activists subscribed to more than one -ism: abolitionism, feminism, evangelism and, as we shall see in the next chapter, spiritualism. Political and social linkages between these groups were significant and fluid. Thus the definition of the term hoodoo, in the popular mind, was expansive. It could include not only root doctors or blacks who practiced the traditions but also their friends and allies who tolerated it, such as the oddball, weird, eccentric types who are often at the forefront of social, political and cultural change. The term might also capture the idea that these people, like spiritualists and faith healers, were engaged in practicing rites and rituals that were beyond the pale, outside the norm, on the fringe.

Rochester, of course, was a crucial center for these types of people and these movements. Whether in 1818 when it was commented on that Rochester had more church pews than residents, that the first antislavery speech ever delivered was in Rochester or that the origins of the women's rights movement, the anti-Masonic movements and, of course, the abolitionist movement were there (as well as Native American shamans, African American root doctors and Baptist faith healers), Rochester was at the center of it all. Hoodoo Corner was its epicenter.

## CHAPTER 10
# The Strange and Tragic Lives of the Fox Sisters

On a cold evening in March 1848, a woman walking down a village street was excitedly accosted by two young girls, new neighbors of hers. The girls told Mary Redfield that since the family had moved into the cottage a few weeks earlier, they'd been hearing odd sounds every night, most especially rapping sounds. Their parents were exhausted and upset, having failed to locate the source of the noise.

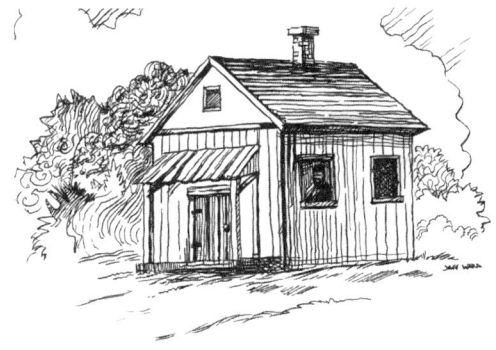

Redfield wondered if it were ghosts or perhaps a childish prank.

A few nights later, John Fox, the father of the girls, appeared at the Redfield cottage. He said that his wife had confirmed that the raps were made by a ghost, apparently the spirit of a man who had been murdered in the cellar of the house. Yet they wanted another opinion. Would Redfield oblige?

When she walked into the east bedroom of the cottage that night, Redfield found Mrs. Fox highly agitated, and the two girls, Kate and Maggie, huddled together in terror on the bed. Mrs. Fox asked, of the thin air: "Are you human?" Two raps sounded. "If you are an injured spirit," Mrs. Fox said, "then count to three." Three raps sounded. Mrs. Fox commanded that the spirit count to five. Five knocks followed.

"By this time," Redfield reported, "I became much interested."

In fact, Mary Redfield was just the first of many who would become "much interested" by the rapping sounds and the Fox sisters. Within days, news of the phenomenon was spreading. Mrs. Fox, in testimony signed four days later, described the events that caused her to send Mr. Fox out for reinforcements that March evening.

She wrote:

> On the night of the first disturbance we all got up, lighted a candle and searched the entire house, the noises continuing during the time and being heard near the same place. Although not very loud, it produced a jar of the bedsteads and chairs that could be felt when we were in bed. It was a tremulous motion, more than a sudden jar. We could feel the jar when standing on the floor. It continued on this night until we slept. I did not sleep until about twelve o'clock. On March 30 we were disturbed all night. The noises were heard in all parts of the house. My husband stationed himself outside the door while I stood inside, and the knocks came on the door between us. We heard footsteps in the pantry, and walking downstairs; we could not rest, and I then concluded that the house must be haunted by some unhappy restless spirit. I had often heard of such things, but had never witnessed anything of the kind that I could not account for before.
>
> On Friday night, March 31, 1848, we concluded to go to bed early and not permit ourselves to be disturbed by the noises, but try and get a night's rest. My husband was here on all these occasions, heard the noises and helped in the search. It was very early when we went to bed on this night—hardly dark. I had been so broken of my rest I was almost sick. My husband had not gone to bed when we first heard the noise on this evening. I had just lain down. It commenced as usual. I knew it from all the other noises I had ever heard before. The children, who slept in the other bed in the room, heard the rapping and tried to make similar sounds by snapping their fingers.
>
> My youngest child said: "Mr. Splitfoot, do as I do," clapping her hands. The sound instantly followed her with the same number of raps. When she stopped the sound ceased for a short time. Then Margareta said, in sport, "No, do just as I do. Count one, two, three, four," striking one hand against the other at the same time; and the raps came as before. She was afraid to repeat them. Then [Kate] said in her childish simplicity, "Oh, mother, I know what it is. Tomorrow is April-fool day and it is somebody trying to fool us." I then thought I could put a test that no one in the place could answer. I asked the noise to rap my different children's ages, successively. Instantly

## The Strange and Tragic Lives of the Fox Sisters

*each one of my children's ages was given correctly, pausing between them sufficiently long to individualize them until the seventh, at which a longer pause was made, and then three more emphatic raps were given, corresponding to the age of the little one that died, which was my youngest child.*

*I then asked: "Is this a human being that answers my questions so correctly?" There was no rap. I asked "Is it a spirit? If it is make two raps." Two sounds were given as soon as the request was made. I then said: "If it was an injured spirit, make two raps," which were instantly made, causing the house to tremble. I asked: "Were you injured in this house?" The answer was given as before. "Is the person living that injured you?" Answered by raps in the same manner, I ascertained by the same simple method that it was a man, aged 31 years, that he had been murdered in this house and his remains were buried in the cellar; that his family consisted of a wife and five children, two sons and three daughters, all living at the time of his death, but that the wife had since died. I asked: 'Will you continue to rap if I call my neighbors that they may hear it too?" The raps were loud in the affirmative.*

Neighbors did come, and would keep on coming. This evening was only the first of many more to follow, with the young Fox girls entrancing, entertaining and befuddling audiences with their ability to communicate with spirits. The question of their psychic abilities, or lack thereof, would

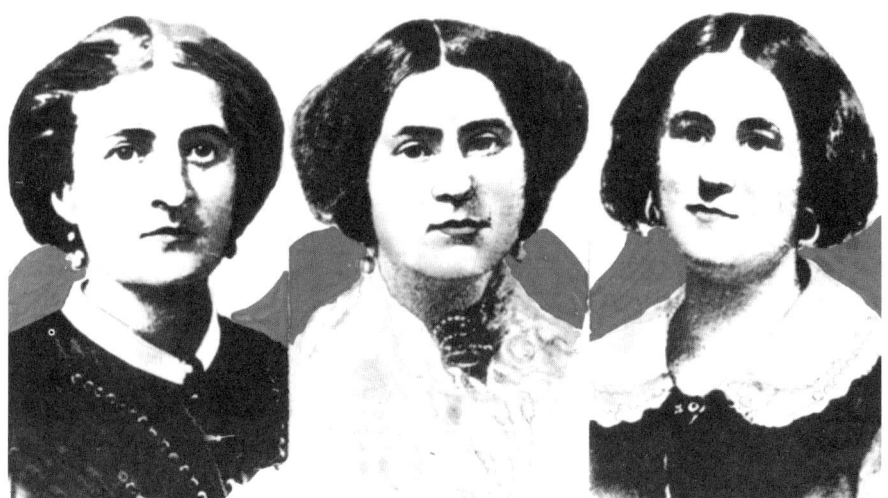

An illustration of the Fox sisters. Maggie and Kate Fox are credited with starting the modern spiritualist movement that, at its zenith, numbered over two million members.

become the major driving force of their lives and gain them a national and international following. They would go on to international stardom, holding public séances in America and Europe. Among their audiences would be people like Horace Greeley, William Cullen Bryant, James Fennimore Cooper, Frederick Douglass, Sojourner Truth and William Lloyd Garrison. Their individual story would become part of a much larger phenomenon, the birth of a new movement called spiritualism, when psychic "mediums" became household names and the investigation of psychic phenomena became widespread. The sisters would draw around them a psychic community, forever changing the landscape of western New York and Rochester. Their life's work, however, would end largely in embarrassment and defeat and ultimately bring as much heartache and destruction to their lives as it did opportunity and success.

\*\*\*

John Fox was born in the 1780s, the son of a blacksmith, and grew up in Rockland County, New York. In 1812, he married sixteen-year old-Margaret Smith. Margaret's family history is difficult to tease out, partly because of the passage of time, partly because it may have been deliberately obscured. It appears that she was descended from a French Huguenot family that switched allegiances from American to British in the midst of the Revolutionary War, an embarrassing past the family might have been inclined to hide. She grew up on the Canadian side of Lake Ontario. Her grandmother, also named Margaret, was something of a legend among her nearby contemporaries, for she was reputed to be blessed with psychic gifts, including the ability to predict the deaths of friends and family. Such a revelation usually came in the vision of a funeral, complete with details of what the deceased would be wearing, who would be in the funeral procession and what the headstone would say.

John and Margaret had four children (perhaps a fifth, who died in infancy) in rapid succession during this period, beginning with Leah in 1813 and ending with David in 1820. Precisely where they lived over the next decade or so is difficult to trace, but the evidence suggests that they moved to western New York during this period, probably drawn, as so many others had been, to the economic possibilities provided by the new Erie Canal.

But the marital relationship foundered, and they separated apparently in the early 1820s, perhaps because John became, in the terminology of the day, a "sporting gentleman." He reportedly took an inordinate interest in alcohol, card-playing and horse racing and found plenty of opportunity to indulge his appetites in the rapidly growing canal towns of that era. Margaret and the children moved in with her spinster sister, who lived in Rochester.

There were other difficulties. At age fourteen, Leah entered into some kind of marriage with a local man—whether legal or de facto isn't clear—but at any rate, she gave birth to a daughter shortly thereafter. She soon enough returned to live with her mother and sisters, a pattern that would repeat in some ways throughout their lives.

In the early 1830s, John reformed his ways, giving up drinking and gambling. He began attending a Methodist church. He and his wife reconciled and moved back across Lake Ontario into Canada. There, they had two more children, Margareta (circa 1833), known as Maggie, and Catherine (circa 1837), known as Kate. Very little is known about their life in Canada. But the family reappears in Rochester-area historical records in the early 1840s. In December 1847, they settled in a small cottage in Hydesville, some thirty miles west of Rochester.

By March of the following year, Maggie and Kate were communicating with a spirit. And word spread quickly. Mrs. Redfield was so unsettled by what she was seeing in the cottage that night that she went immediately to get her husband. After hearing the rappings, he went to get a neighboring couple, the Dueslers. They, in turn, called in other neighbors. Some men who happened to be passing by the cottage that night became curious about the hubbub and were welcomed in, becoming witnesses as well.

Mr. Duesler, who had briefly lived in the cottage many years before, took the lead in questioning the spirit. With Maggie serving as the primary interpreter, it was revealed through a series of raps that the man was a peddler who had visited the cottage about five years before. He had been murdered in the bedroom of the cottage by the then tenant, John Bell. The peddler's throat had been cut with a butcher knife. The spirit was quite specific, communicating even that he'd been killed on a Tuesday at midnight. The motive was apparently robbery. The peddler/spirit claimed that he had been carrying $500, which was then more than a working man's annual wages. His body, he said, was then taken down to the cellar, though he was not buried until the next night, about ten feet below the surface of the ground.

In addition to answering questions about his life and death, the spirit revealed a certain familiarity with the neighborhood. He was quizzed about some of the families in Hydesville, particularly the numbers of children in each. He always responded with the correct number of raps. The spirit generally answered yes-or-no questions (a rap for yes, silence for no), but in one complicated and time-consuming exchange, letters of the alphabet were indicated by a given number of raps, and the spirit revealed that his initials included a C and a B.

Eventually, Mr. Redfield, holding a candle, went into the cellar to search for a possible grave. Directed from above, through questions posed by Mr. Duesler, asked of the spirit by Maggie and answered by raps from the spirit, Mr. Redfield was guided time and again to a certain spot on the dirt floor of the cellar.

By midnight, the girls and Mrs. Fox were exhausted and left the cottage to spend the night with friends. Mr. Fox and Mr. Redfield kept watch in the house overnight, while the neighbors dispersed.

When Mr. Duesler arrived the next evening, he found a crowd of nearly one hundred people in and around the house. Most of the action was taking place in the same small bedroom, where the girls once again sat on the bed and where the rappings had resumed. Later that evening, some of the men descended into the cellar and dug up the floor, hoping to find the peddler's grave. They were forced to stop when they'd dug about three feet into the floor and water began to rise.

The situation continued much the same on the following days. Crowds were drawn to the house, and men worked in the cellar, unsuccessful in their quest to find the skeleton of the peddler. Various committees were formed and staked out other areas on the property, alert for any unusual activity. Others searched the house, looking for alternate explanations for the noises.

Some observers took the opportunity to ask the spirit questions about their own concerns. Duesler, for instance, queried the spirit on the relative merits of Universalist and Methodist doctrines. From the raps, it was clear that the spirit sided with the Methodists.

Mary Redfield asked the spirit if there was really such a thing as heaven, and it responded in the affirmative. When she asked if her own daughter, Mary, was there, the spirit likewise responded affirmatively.

## Reports of Mysterious Noises

### *Fame Begins*

Local papers picked up on the story and began reporting by early April. It didn't take long for doubts to arise. A doctor who was called to attend to Kate, who had taken ill, reported that he heard the raps—that they had been coming from all around the bed—but that he couldn't locate their source. He believed, he told his daughter, that the girls were making the noises themselves, by "some way manipulating the joints or muscles of the fingers, toes, and knees." Others accused the Foxes of blasphemy.

Then the Weekmans, who had lived in the cottage a year before, came forward to say that they had heard mysterious rappings as well. A boarder who had lived in the house even earlier claimed to have seen a specter in the house, who wore "grey pants, black frock coat, and black cap." Finally, a nineteen-year-old woman, Lucretia Pulver, stepped forward with some crucial details.

She had worked for the Bells, who'd lived in the cottage some years before, and according to her, one evening a foot peddler had appeared at the door. The peddler carried a trunk and a basket. The next morning, the Bells sent Lucretia away for a few days, and when she came back to work, there was no sign of the peddler, but Mrs. Bell asked her to mend two coats that had been ripped. Although Lucretia never saw the peddler again, over the next few months, Mrs. Bell had sometimes claimed that the man still visited and showed Lucretia small items, thimbles or other doodads, that a peddler might carry in his trunk.

Within weeks of the event, E.E. Lewis, an attorney and reporter from nearby Canandaigua, collected depositions from twenty locals about the events in the cottage and published a pamphlet with his findings. Most of his witnesses began by denying a belief in the supernatural and then recounted their experiences, admitting to being baffled and ultimately being unable to discount the supernatural provenance of the sounds. Lewis included testimony from friends and neighbors of the Bells as well, all of whom stated that he was of good character, and they did not believe that he had murdered the peddler. Lewis did not, however, take statements from the young girls, Kate and Maggie, at the center of the story.

* * *

In April 1848, Leah Fox was living in Rochester, and hearing of the goings-on in Hydesville, she made her way to her family's home. She found the "spook house," the name already attached to the cottage by reporters, deserted. Leah then made her way to her brother's farm, where she found her parents and the girls. Mrs. Fox had turned grey with the strain of the previous month, and Mr. Fox was busily constructing a home next to his son's.

But the crowds had followed the family and milled around outside, now and then looking inside the windows of the farmhouse. The move had not solved the problem of the spirit either, for he had seemed to follow the girls to their new abode. He had recently, for instance, revealed that his name was Charles B. Rosna.

Leah decided that the best approach to calming things down was to separate the girls. She therefore decided to take Kate to stay with her for awhile, put her in the carriage and headed back to Rochester. She found, however, that after only a few "miles on the canal…we became aware that the rapping had accompanied us." Back at the farm, where Maggie remained, the sounds continued apace, with the spirit trying as well to communicate through Maggie.

Kate's first weeks in Rochester were very difficult. The first spirit seemed to have been joined by others, and they were out of control, behaving as poltergeists. The disturbances occurred primarily at night, with the sounds of clog dancing, furniture being moved about and doors being open and shut. Leah soon took her own young daughter and Kate and abandoned the house in Rochester. Leah rented another home in Rochester, and after a few quiet nights, Mrs. Fox and Maggie arrived for a visit.

Apparently, with the family reunited, the spirits returned in force. In her memoirs, Leah recounts teasing one of the spirits who was making dancing sounds, inquiring "Flatfoot, can you dance the Highland fling?" Mrs. Fox was horrified. There was also an unusually frightening evening, during which the spirits seemed to slap members of the family in turn, hitting Kate so hard that she fell to the floor, the wind knocked out of her.

In June 1848, a Congregational minister who was traveling through Rochester stopped at the house. Lemuel Clark was outraged by what he believed to be a fraud being perpetrated on the community. Clark was bothered not only on religious grounds but particularly because a local friend had recounted to him a story about being contacted by the spirit of his dead daughter, Harriet. Clark saw this as preying on the grief of the man and intended to debunk the stories of the Fox sisters.

Thus the Fox family was invited to a gathering of some twenty people in the parlor of a friend's home, and Clark began the visit with a prayer. He had no sooner begun speaking than he was interrupted by rapping sounds. Soon enough, the assembled crowd was asking questions of the spirits and receiving answers. Clark demanded that everyone push their chairs together in a circle, feet on the rungs, hands in the air. He then commanded the spirits to move the table. The table slid about a foot toward him. Then it moved

# The Strange and Tragic Lives of the Fox Sisters

back. Clark later examined the table, looking for hidden wires or some other physical mechanism to explain its movement. He found none.

Clark met with the family twice more during this visit, and the unexplainable events continued apace. In one heartrending moment, Clark witnessed Lizzie, Leah's daughter, being berated by the assembled group for voicing a wish that the spirits would leave, that she was afraid of what might happen to her mother, her grandmother and her aunts, Kate and Maggie. The scene ended horribly, with the crying little girl being forced to beg for forgiveness from the spirits and her family. She was shortly thereafter sent to live with her father in Illinois.

These evenings with a group communicating with spirits were the beginning of the pattern that would characterize the life of the Fox sisters for some years to come. They regularly began to hold such events, known as spirit circles, sittings or séances. The meetings were held in private houses with a limited number of attendees. There were rappings, questions asked of the spirits, and furniture being moved about. Kate was the primary medium, the chosen vehicle through which the spirits communicated.

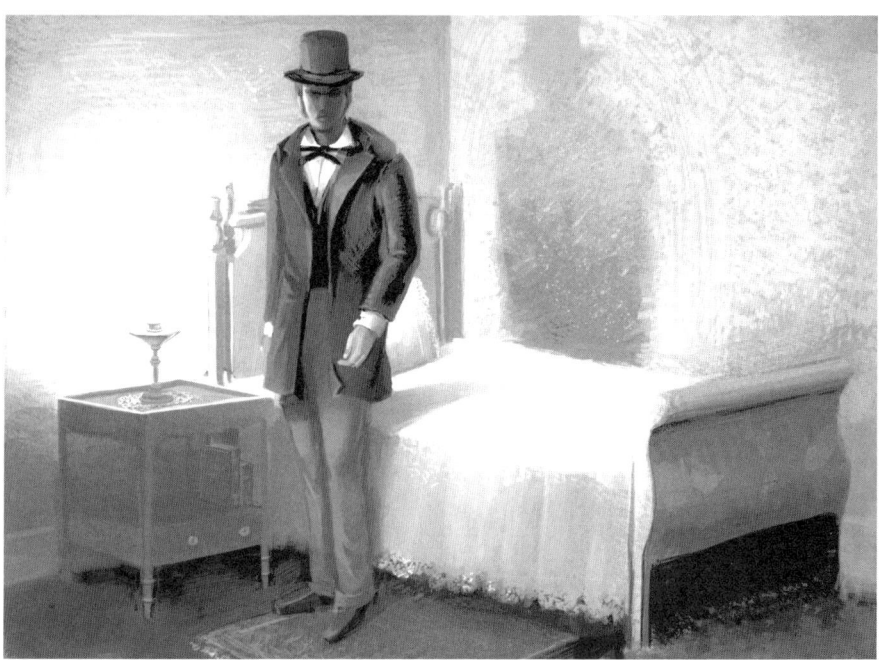

An illustration of peddler Charles B. Rosna. Fifty years after a report of the first rapping sounds, a newspaper reported that a skeleton was found buried in the cellar of the Fox cottage.

In July 1848, the Fox family traveled back to Hydesville with the primary aim of uncovering the remains of the spirit/peddler, Charles B. Rosna. Though they did not find a skeleton and had continued trouble with water flooding into the areas they dug, they did find smashed bits of pottery, strands of hair and bone fragments. For many skeptics, this was not enough evidence to prove the assertions of the Fox sisters, though for many others, those who were on the border between skepticism and belief, it seemed to cement their belief in the Fox girls. Other skeptics, however, became more openly hostile at this point, as if the discovery were a call to arms. One night, a threatening crowd gathered outside the family farm. Many of the men brought firearms with them. Among the primary agitators were friends of Mr. Bell. Others were Christians who feared that the devil himself might be involved in the events around the Fox girls.

The potential for violence was real. From the Salem witch trials in the eighteenth century right down to the case of Joseph Smith, who had been murdered by a hostile crowd only four years earlier, some Americans had shown a propensity to respond with violence when there were perceived threats to established religion. The Foxes once again decamped to Rochester.

## Skepticism and Resistance

As Kate and Maggie Fox became more well known and drew more prominent adherents, they likewise drew more formidable opponents. Many people appointed themselves investigators of a sort and took on the task of proving the girls a fraud. As Clark did, many searched for physical explanations: some skeptics searched for wires and mechanical devices, while others carefully watched for signals between the girls and other members of the family during the séances. Some skeptics concentrated on investigating the spirits: asking a variety of questions, some leading, some trick, designed specifically to trip them up. Others asked the spirits for minor details: where were you born? Where did you die? What were you wearing when you died? Eliab Capron, a relative of the well-known mesmerism researcher Dr. George Capron, found that the spirits could answer questions not only posed aloud but also those only asked mentally or written on a piece of paper.

In the fall of 1849, the course of events changed dramatically. Though the Fox sisters were still routinely visited by skeptics and believers, religious folks who tried to save them, investigators and the merely curious, they now had difficulty from an unexpected quarter: the spirits themselves. The spirits had been demanding for some time that the Fox girls take the truth of immortality and the very presence of the spirits around them to the public at large. Until this moment, the fame of the Fox girls was confined more or less to western New York. But one afternoon, their entreaties apparently ignored too long, the spirits delivered an ultimatum: "We will now bid you all farewell."

And so they did. The house went quiet. No rapping, tapping or overturned furniture. A few weeks later, George Willets and Capron arrived for a visit and found Maggie and Leah dejected by the quiet, by the absence of the spirits. Capron suggested that perhaps the spirits would rap for him, and indeed, suddenly, they did. But they had a demand: "You have a duty to perform. We want you to make this matter more public." The spirits insisted that their truth be shared publicly.

And so they got their wish. Willets, Capron, the Posts and others began a flurry of activity, drafting lectures, holding practice sessions with invited guests and organizing the business end of things. Finally, on November 14, 1849, the girls gave their first appearance in a public venue at Rochester's Corinthian Hall. The crowd numbered nearly four hundred. Capron delivered a lecture on the history of events to date, and the spirits accompanied Maggie and Leah (Kate was absent) onto the stage, providing a consistent background noise of knocks and raps. At the end of the evening, a committee of audience members was formed to investigate the phenomenon.

An even larger crowd met the following evening at the Sons of Temperance Hall to hear the results of the investigation. They were shocked to hear that the men, after attending two events with the girls, could find no earthly explanation for the raps, and that the experiments designed to trip up the girls and the spirits were unsuccessful. The crowd appointed another committee of five men to try again. This time, the group included the vice chancellor of New York state, Frederick Whittlesey. The investigation included the girls being physically examined by a doctor. The results, reported to a crowd at Corinthian Hall the next evening, were substantially the same. Yet a third committee was appointed, this time with one wrinkle: it included a ladies' committee that was tasked with stripping the girls and searching them. Maggie and Leah Fox submitted, though both wept through it. Again, no physical explanation or devices were found that could explain the sounds.

By Saturday afternoon, the situation was growing tense and perhaps dangerous. Some of Rochester's citizens were outraged, asserting that the committees weren't objective. Others accused the participants, including the Fox sisters, their friends and allies and even the audience, of blasphemy. Many were offended by women appearing onstage and by the physical examinations of the Fox sisters, which had to be discussed publicly in order for the findings to be presented. The Fox sisters nevertheless appeared at the hall, despite being exhausted and fearful. Josiah Bissel, a devout Christian, distributed firecrackers among the audience and the series of explosions disrupted the event. The girls were escorted to safety by the police chief.

Bissel's efforts perhaps backfired because he ensured a high level of publicity. And, as grueling as the events had been, the sisters found themselves with proof, of a sort, of their legitimacy. Willets and Capron wrote an article summarizing the events, which was published in the *New York Tribune*. The girls were now famous beyond the boundaries of Rochester and of western New York, and they would endure both the benefits and costs that fame inevitably seems to bring.

\*\*\*

Early in 1850, the Fox sisters began holding séances in public venues. They were now a permanent threesome, with Leah acting as a sort of emcee to events, while Kate, now twelve, and Maggie, now sixteen, interceded with the spirits. The séances were very popular, often drawing standing-room only crowds in Rochester.

The personal story of the Fox sisters was now intersecting with wider cultural developments in this decade. This was an era of the rise of science and of the fantastic as well. So-called "mediums" became numerous, and the investigation of spiritualist and psychic phenomena interested many. Phrenology was in vogue, the telegraph was recently invented and P.T. Barnum had begun to present his shows of human curiosities. The first experimental spiritualist organization, the New York Circle, was formed in 1851. According to a then new periodical, *Spirit World*, by 1851, there were one hundred mediums in New York and fifty spirit circles in Philadelphia. By 1855, the New England Spiritualist Association counted nearly two million spiritualists in the United States, an assertion that was backed up by independent journalists. Topical periodicals flourished: the *Univercoelum*, the *Spirit Messenger*, the *Spiritual and Moral Instructor*, *Heat and Light*, the *Spiritual Philosopher*, *Shekinah* and the *Spiritual Telegraph* were just a few of the magazines and newspapers born in this period.

Eliab Capron was deeply interested in the subject, and he wrote and published on it. He continued to orbit around the girls, and he soon asked

Mrs. Fox if he could take the girls to New York City for a demonstration of their skills. She initially resisted. Meanwhile, the Fox sisters took part in another event at Corinthian Hall in the spring of 1850, and it went well. They attended another in Albany and then another in Troy, New York. By June 1850, Mrs. Fox's resistance had worn down, and the girls were checking into Barnum's Hotel on Broadway.

The sessions they held there were attended by all kinds of people, including doctors, lawyers, businessmen and journalists, including Horace Greeley. Famous people attended as well, such as James Fennimore Cooper, William Cullen Bryant, George Bancroft and Jenny Lind, the so-called Swedish Nightingale, among others. The sessions became so well known that a Broadway singer wrote a song about them: "The Rochester Knockings at Barnum's Hotel."

The atmosphere was much like it had been in Rochester, with repeated attempts to uncover any fraud that might be at work: trick questioning, examination of the room and the items in it and the girls themselves. By the end of the summer, Greeley had become convinced of the authenticity of the Fox sisters and published a strong article to that effect.

He wrote:

> *Whatever may be the origin or the cause of the "rappings," the ladies in whose presence they occur do not make them. We tested this thoroughly, and to our satisfaction. Their conduct and bearing is as unlike that of deceivers as possible; and we think no one once acquainted with them could believe them at all capable of engaging in so daring, impious, and shameful a juggle as this would be if they caused the sounds. And it is not possible that such a juggle should have been so long perpetuated in public.*

Greeley was, in fact, so taken with the girls that he extended an offer for Kate to live with his family and get a good education at a girl's academy in New York City. She accepted the offer, while Leah and Maggie returned to Rochester. Kate was apparently miserable there, however, complaining in letters home about Mrs. Greeley, the school, and frequent headaches. In fact, the rather peripatetic existence that the family had already lived—as landlords and neighbors tired of the disruptions caused by the spirits and registered their protests, causing the family to move back and forth across Lake Ontario from the United States to Canada; in New York, among Rochester, Hydesville and the family farm; and even among dwellings in Rochester—seemed now to accelerate.

The separations took a toll. Mrs. Fox seems to have been overwhelmed in the attempt to manage her family, with pressures exerted not only by Leah and the younger girls but also by the friends and hangers-on who gathered around the girls. Everyone had their own opinion about how best to manage the situation and/or take advantage of it, and most were not afraid to voice it. There was constant discussion about how to handle one thing or another—whether to take an engagement, how to manage the disruptive spirits, how to respond to a skeptic's charges—and the cost to the two young girls at the center of it all became more apparent in this period. Both girls had always complained of headaches and other physical ailments, and from this period, the stresses seem to have become a more-or-less permanent theme in their lives.

In November 1850, seventeen-year-old Maggie went alone to Troy, New York, for an event. She was followed and harassed there by a group of men. They followed her during the day, spied on her at night, threw a stone at her and then threw stones at the house she was staying in. Then they broke into the house. The family she was staying with protected her, hid her away in a small bedroom and then telegraphed Leah to come and get her. Leah arrived to find the owner of the home brandishing a pistol against the mob that had formed outside the home. Leah found Maggie sobbing and vomiting from fear. They eventually made it to Albany and back to Rochester, where they returned to holding séances.

But it was clear now that the risks were growing as these young women challenged not only deeply entrenched religious values but societal notions of the proper place for women as well. The Fox sisters were, in some ways, an anomaly; all three were young and financially independent, earning their own money. They had no apparent need of a man to provide for them. Although there were men around them—their father, various supporters and advisors—they were not seen to be firmly under the control of any of them, much less a husband. As research on many witch trials has shown, those most likely to find themselves charged with that activity were single, independent women. It was a challenge that, to traditional society, could be dangerous.

In the same way, spiritualism challenged religious organizations and hierarchies. Spiritualism is the belief that death is only the end of the physical body, and the spirit continues on in other planes of existence. Some claim that there are various levels of these planes, with each presenting a higher level of growth and perfection, and that spirits thus continue to grow and develop, achieving higher levels of perfection. But the central belief is that the spirits of the dead can and do communicate with living people and are capable of providing valuable information about God, life on earth (particularly in regard to moral and ethical issues) and life in the spirit world. And such spirits communicate directly with individuals, often through a medium. But mediums are not trained or controlled by any central authority.

In the same way, there is not one central spiritualist text nor is there any monopoly on interpreting those that do exist, such as there is in established religions. Rather, there are many commonly held tenets, including the belief that God is expressed through nature, that individuals never truly die and that true religion is expressed in following the law of nature. Though spiritualism clearly does not exclude a belief in God, neither does it emphasize the Christian Bible, the Judeo-Christian concept of God, the concept of sin or organized structures such as the church. Thus the Fox sisters and spiritualism constituted a direct challenge to existing religious notions and institutions, which made them targets for those who opposed change in these areas.

One person who was particularly interested in spiritualism for precisely these reasons was Susan B. Anthony. She was born into a Quaker family in 1820 and had led a somewhat restricted childhood, although her family belonged to a liberal Society of Friends. Nevertheless, Anthony became aware of the inequalities between men and women at a young age and was particularly concerned with economic inequality. She fought for equal wages for women as a young teacher in New York. As her interest in women's rights grew, she spent a great deal of time traveling the country and lecturing, often with fellow advocate Elizabeth Cady Stanton.

Like most activists, her friends and acquaintances were political reformers like herself, fellow sometimes outcasts like Douglass and other radical abolitionists. Anthony separated herself from the religion of her childhood as she matured and, eventually, from Christianity. She believed it to be intolerably oppressive to women. Though she was never a formal member of any spiritualist group, she recognized it as a rare religion that did not subjugate women. In a lecture she gave at Lily Dale, a community formed by and for spiritualists, she said: "The only religious sect in the world…that has recognized the equality of women is the spiritualists."[42]

To be fair, however, it must be noted that some of the hostility toward the Fox sisters came not on the basis of their challenge to existing social and political norms but over the simple issue of truth. Many believed them to be frauds, plain and simple. One such opponent was Stanley Grimes, a well-known lecturer on spiritualism and phrenology. Another committed antagonist and determined skeptic was C. Chauncey Burr, a lawyer and

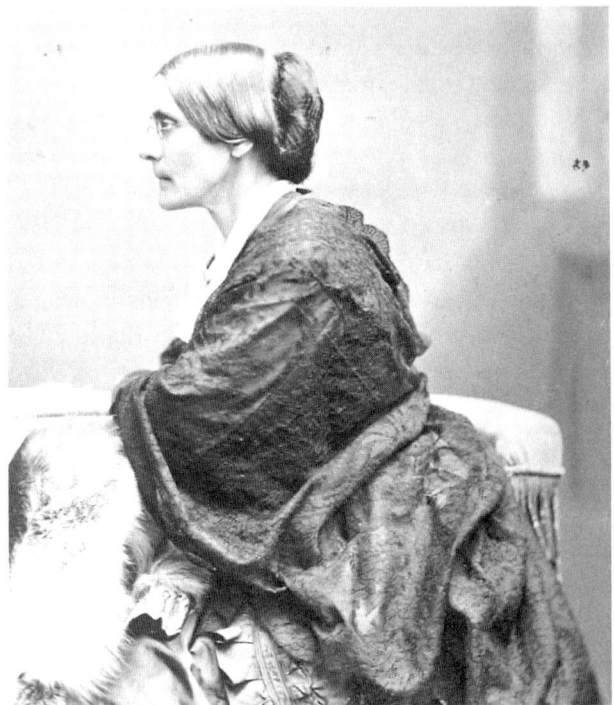

Susan B. Anthony, 1820–1906, was a proponent and leader of the women's rights movement. Few knew of her relationship with the Fox sisters and the spiritualism movement. *Courtesy of Rochester Public Library.*

Universalist minister. These two were involved in a plan to expose the girls. Under some pressure, Kate and Maggie submitted to an examination by a committee of three professors from the University of Buffalo. The men were not able to conclusively prove the girls a fraud, but the general tone of the report was insulting and dismissive. Maggie responded in print and offered a challenge. Another series of grueling examinations occurred, with the men asking questions of the spirits while taking turns holding the legs of the girls or having the girls sit or stand in a variety of positions intended to prevent them from making the sounds with their joints. There were certain positions that indeed seemed to slow or prevent the rapping entirely. But the Fox sisters had a response, saying that the spirits were sometimes tired themselves and did not perform, or, perhaps, the spirits were offended by the actions of the men.

The "battle in Buffalo" drew renewed public interest, and crowds once again gathered around the house where the girls were staying. Leah waived the fee for entrance to a séance for a week or so, and the numbers continued to grow. Although the battle ended, in scientific terms, in a draw, it was a resounding public success for the girls. They left Buffalo in the spring with a tidy financial profit.

# The Strange and Tragic Lives of the Fox Sisters

A few weeks later, Burr published a deposition of the testimony of a distant relative of Kate's. The woman, Mrs. Norman Culver, claimed that she had approached Kate and baited her with questions, asking about how to conduct a successful séance. Kate told her that the key to making the rapping sounds was in using the joints of the toes. Kate reportedly gave an entire primer, saying that the key to answering questions depended on reading the facial expressions and body language of those who were doing the asking, or knew the answers, for clues as to when the right answer was reached. To make the rappings appear to come from a distant place, Kate made the sounds louder and "direct my own eyes earnestly where I wished them to be heard."

Once again, however, the exposé had little effect on the popularity of the girls. They continued to travel farther, heading to Cleveland, Cincinnati and Columbus, Ohio, in 1851. In 1852, they performed in Philadelphia. And in 1853, the Fox sisters permanently moved to New York City.

\*\*\*

For the rest of their lives, the Fox sisters earned their living by communing with spirits. Spiritualism became mainstream, if still a subculture, and the Fox sisters were no longer breaking boundaries so much as living within now wider ones. They were grand dames in the movement, traveling all over the United States and in Europe as well. Maggie eventually married Elisha Kane, an Arctic explorer, and she later converted to Roman Catholicism. Kate married a barrister she met in London, lived there for a time and had two sons. Leah married again, this time into a wealthy family. And over these same years, the relationship among the three women became more and more strained. The younger women seemed to resent Leah, who had always "bossed" them around. There were arguments over money; there were periods of estrangement.

Whether it was cause or effect of these difficulties, Kate and Maggie both developed serious drinking problems. Some claimed that the girls, in fact, began drinking wine at a young age in the absence of consistent parenting and as a method of coping with stress. Others have suggested that alcoholism, or other substance abuse, is a particular danger for such sensitive souls as mediums, who might sometimes have difficulty turning off, or tuning out, the psychic noise around them.

At any rate, by the 1880s, a crisis developed around these issues that once again put the Fox sisters and events at the Hydesville cottage firmly in the public eye. Kate and Maggie were involved in a dispute with their sister Leah and other leading spiritualists who were concerned that Kate was drinking too much to care properly for her children. At the same time, Maggie, perhaps struggling with her own alcoholism and wishing to return to her Christian faith, became concerned about her own role in advocating spiritualism.

## A Celebrated Medium Says the Spirits Never Return

In the fall of 1888, Maggie gave an interview to a reporter for the *New York Herald*. The article recounted the Hydesville events and gave Maggie's explanation of them. She confessed to being a fraud: "When spiritualism first began, Katie and I were little children, and this old woman, my other sister, made us her tools. Mother was a silly woman. She was a fanatic....she believed in those things. Our sister used us in her exhibitions, and we made money for her." Maggie was quite direct in citing Leah's role in these events, accusing her of manipulating the young girls and explaining how some sounds were made by Leah, courtesy of a string tied to an apple. Maggie also reportedly shocked the reporter by demonstrating her own method for making the rapping sounds.

There were, and are, some who believe that Maggie's confession was false or perhaps coerced. The reporter was said to have offered her $1,500 if she would "expose" the methods of the Fox sisters and give him an exclusive on the story. Some believe that Maggie was in desperate need of money at the time, which is supported by some evidence, while others see her as a sick old woman, entering the late stages of alcoholism and perhaps suffering from the cognitive decline that often accompanies this. Others cite the estrangement from Leah and years of resentment built up, particularly over finances. Still others maintain that the Catholic church, through Catholic Charities—which was involved in caring for Kate's children as she battled alcoholism—had some role in the affair and were in effect threatening to take away Kate's children permanently unless the confession was made.

At any rate, Maggie's "confession" drew attention, and she then appeared at the New York Academy of Music on October 21, 1888, with Kate in attendance. Before an audience of two thousand, Maggie demonstrated how she produced the raps, which were audible throughout the theater. Doctors from the audience came on stage to verify that the cracking of her toe joints was the source of the sound.

Maggie gave a thorough description of the method, stating that after the events in Hydesville, the girls were taken to Rochester, where:

> *we discovered a new way to make the raps. My sister Katie was the first to observe that by swishing her fingers she could produce certain noises with her knuckles and joints, and that the same effect could be made with the toes. Finding that we could make raps with our feet—first with one foot and then with both—we practiced until we could do this easily when the room was dark. Like most perplexing things when made clear, it is astonishing how easily it is done. The rappings are simply the result of a perfect control of the muscles of the leg below the knee, which govern the tendons of the foot and allow action of the toe and ankle bones that is not commonly known. Such perfect control is only possible when the child is taken at an early age and carefully and continually taught to practice the muscles, which grow stiffer in later years. This, then, is the simple explanation of the whole method of the knocks and raps.*

Maggie also commented on the tendency of audiences to accept the sounds as true:

> *A great many people when they hear the rappings imagine at once that the spirits are touching them. It is a very common delusion. Some very wealthy people came to see me some years ago when I lived in Forty-second Street and I did some rappings for them. I made the spirit rap on the chair and one of the ladies cried out: "I feel the spirit tapping me on the shoulder." Of course that was pure imagination.*

The reaction was perhaps less than Maggie expected, for those who believed in spiritualism continued to believe, and those who didn't continued not to. But Maggie would soon recant her confession, in any case, in November of the following year. It is not clear why. Again, there is speculation that the crisis involving the Catholic church and Kate's children passed or simply that Maggie felt less inclined to help her sister. Kate refused to speak publicly about the issue at all. Her letters to Maggie after the initial confession express shock and dismay at her sister's attack on spiritualism, but she never made any statement about the substance of Maggie's confession. One possible motive for Maggie's recanting of her confession was offered by John Mulholland, a magician and debunker, who noted wryly: "It was expected that this [the confession] would give her sufficient income to live on, but she shortly discovered that while many people will pay to be humbugged few will pay to be educated."[43]

When the reaction to this event died down shortly thereafter, the story of the Fox sisters had largely come to an end, and in some ways, so had spiritualism. At its height, the movement had several million followers. But by the 1880s, many had lost interest, as it had become tainted by claims and even proof, in some instances, of fraud. The movement would continue on into the twentieth century, when the religion came to be known as the Spiritualist Church, and today, members are counted in over thirty countries.

Nevertheless, the decline of spiritualism coincided with that of its central figures, the Fox sisters. Leah died on November 1, 1890. Kate returned again from England shortly thereafter and took a small apartment in New York City. She died on July 2, 1892. She had apparently been on an extended drinking binge just prior to her death, and the cause of death was determined to be nephritis. There were no funds available to bury her, so her body was placed in a temporary vault. Maggie died on March 8, 1893, of heart failure. Some friends got together and raised money for burial of the Fox sisters. Kate's body was removed from vault and buried, along with Maggie's, in Cypress Hills Cemetery in Brooklyn.

## Postscript

As we've seen with each of our stories, however, they don't end just because their principal characters die. This is true in the case of the Fox sisters as well. They, for instance, lived on in popular culture in ways that most of us would not recognize. L. Frank Baum, the author of *The Wizard of Oz*, was born just a few years after the Foxes first heard the rapping sounds, and he grew up in a small town about one hundred miles from Rochester. One of his biographers has shown that Baum's creation of the Tin Man, the Cowardly Lion and the Scarecrow grew out of the spiritualist movement swirling around him. In fact, he traces Baum's signature creation, Dorothy's heel-clicking of her ruby red slippers in order to get home, to the question of whether the Fox sisters made the rapping sounds by clicking the joints of their feet.[44]

There were also dramatic follow-up events. In November 1904, a skeleton was discovered in the cellar of the Hydesville cottage in which the Fox sisters first heard the rappings. William Hyde, the owner of the cottage, reported finding the bones after a cellar wall collapsed, being undermined by underground running water.[45] Nearly fifty years earlier, Maggie and Kate had claimed that they had established communication with the spirit of a peddler, Charles B. Rosna, who claimed to have been murdered and buried in the cellar. Was this him? Could this be proof, finally, that the Fox sisters had been telling the truth?

The *Boston Journal* reported the incident:

> *The skeleton of the man who first caused the rappings heard by the Fox Sisters…has been found between the walls of the house occupied by the sisters, and clears them from the only shadow of doubt held concerning their discovery of spirit communication. The discovery was made by school children playing in the cellar of the building in Hydesville known as "The Spook House," where the Fox sisters first heard the wonderful rappings. A reputable citizen of Clyde, who owns the house, made an investigation, and found an almost entire human skeleton between the crumbling walls, undoubtedly that of the wandering peddler who it was claimed was murdered in the east room and buried in the basement.*

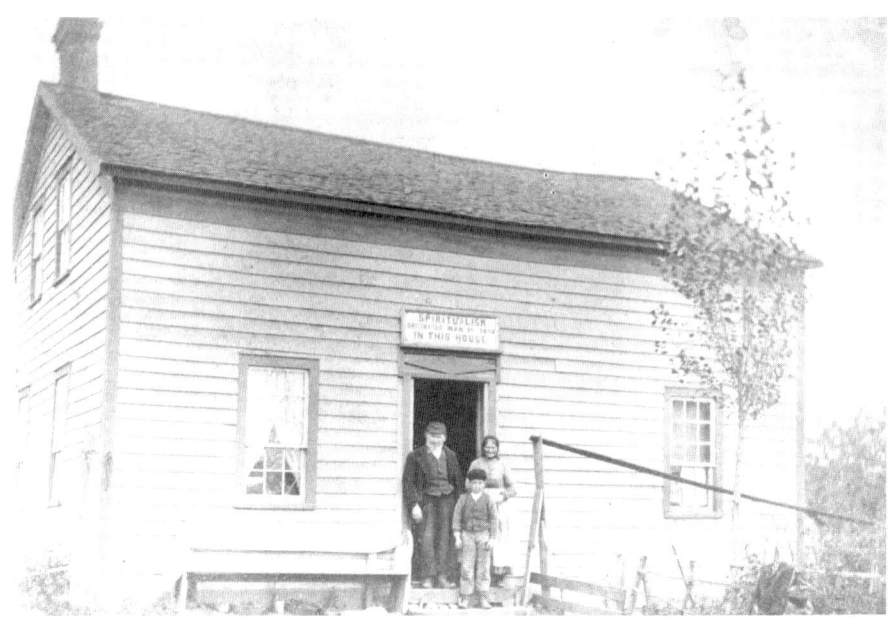

The Fox sisters' cottage in Hydesville. It was here that the girls claimed to have heard "rapping" sounds from the spirit of a dead man believed to have been murdered in the cottage. *Courtesy of Rochester Public Library.*

> *Examination revealed that a false and unobserved inner wall had been built. Between this false inner wall and the original outer wall and near the center of the basement, the skeleton was found. It is interesting to know that the false wall is composed of stones like those used fifty years ago to build stone fences. This recalls a statement made over fifty years ago by Miss Lucretia Pulver that Mr. Bell* [the earlier house owner and presumed murderer] *worked each night under cover of darkness, carrying stones from the fence into the cellar. The finding of the bones corroborates the sworn statement made by Margaret Fox.*[46]

Does it? In short, we don't know. There certainly is no definitive proof that the bones are of a murdered peddler, when they were buried or even that all of the bones are human. Like everything else about the Fox sisters, there are claims and counterclaims, and the dispute goes on.[47]

What is clear is that there was still passion around the issue even a decade after the deaths of the women involved. The Fox sisters had helped create and popularize an entire movement that, in fact, changed the spiritual geography of western New York.

## CONCLUSION
# The Legend of Hoodoo Corner

A modern-day visitor to Rochester can find Hoodoo Corner quite easily; it is marked by the Liberty Pole. That is a little misleading, perhaps, because that site has been the home of a series of Liberty Poles, the first of which was erected in 1830. There have been at least five different Liberty Poles erected there. Initially, they were made of hickory or ash and later iron or steel. Each of them eventually needed to be replaced, as a result of the passage of time and/or natural disaster, like a lightning storm, a windstorm or simple aging. Banners or flags were often hung from them to celebrate holidays and national victories, such as the Fourth of July, the Mexican War and the Civil War. The most recent Liberty Pole went up in the 1960s, and it is a prominent landmark, serving as the site for rallies, war protests and political campaigns.[48]

It is interesting to note that the Liberty Pole is a kind of man-made hoodoo in the geographical sense of the word. It is a tall, thin structure that stands out from the geography around it. Hoodoos, in the natural world, are formed over a long period of time—geologic time, in fact. The oddly shaped pedestals of earth or pillars of rock develop through erosion by wind and water, especially in areas where the sedimentary layers alternate between soft and hard material. Thus, any hoodoo in a canyon is in fact not one simple thing but the result of a long series of events and processes that gave rise to it.

In a legend of the Paiute Indians, who inhabited the Bryce Canyon area for hundreds of years before the arrival of European Americans, hoodoos are said to be "Legend People" who were turned to stone as punishment for bad deeds.[49] In Blackfoot mythology, hoodoos were giants whom the Great Spirit had turned to stone because of their evil deeds. Deep in the night, it is said that the petrified giants can awaken and throw down boulders upon any humans passing nearby.[50] Over time, the term hoodoo came be used to refer to any malignant creature or evil supernatural force.

In the same way that such Indian legends account for long and complicated natural processes and the daily vagaries of human existence, Rochester's Legend of Hoodoo Corner accounts for a long, complex and sometimes inexplicable series of human events. How much simpler, though less interesting, it would be, of course, if there were a single explanation for the legend of Hoodoo Corner, one single historic event that explains how there came to be a belief that the corner was cursed. But there isn't a single, simple answer to the question of how it acquired its name.

It was rather a slow accretion of details, beliefs, events and reactions to those events. When Colonel Nathaniel Rochester arrived at the spot that would become Hoodoo Corner in 1800, it was simply the intersection of Indian trails with a burial ground nearby. Within twenty years, the first building had been raised there, and Rochester soon became the fastest-growing city in the young nation, drawing a vast influx of new people and new ideas to the city via the Erie Canal. Many of the new people were immigrants, while others were simply migrants who brought with them different religions, customs and beliefs. Rapid economic development was matched by profound social unease and with an explosion of religious experimentation that would soon give way to new movements, like women's rights, abolitionism and spiritualism.

The historical record suggests that though there were a number of actual historic events that happened near that intersection in Rochester, the meaning of the legend of Hoodoo Corner is, in the end, metaphorical. It describes, by reference to a particular location, many of the broader social and political forces at work in the city and region and captures the fear and wonderment engendered by this period of rapid social, political, economic, religious and racial change. There must often have been the sense that many foreign, dark and mysterious things were happening in such a rapidly changing world.

There often seemed to be a widespread sense that reality, what was really happening, was in some senses hidden from the naked eye. From the disappearance of Captain William Morgan, to the supposed machinations of the Freemasons—and not only in the Morgan case but in local political life—to the rapping sounds in the home of the Fox sisters, there was a

## The Legend of Hoodoo Corner

perhaps overwhelming sense that things were not quite what they appeared. And this was often true. Because of its geographic location, as well as the beliefs of many of its citizens, Rochester was a critical point on the Underground Railroad. Many residents took part in moving slaves from the south, housing them in churches and homes scattered around Rochester, and then moving them across the Niagara River to freedom in Canada. The average Rochester citizen would not be incorrect in having the feeling that, while they slept, secret things were going on in the town.

The metaphorical sense of the word captures as well the fear and unease engendered by the presence of the "other." From Rochester's earliest days, when Handsome Lake and the Seneca lived a stone's throw away, the city was a nearly perpetual crossroads in American life, demonstrated in the influx of Catholics, French speakers, Germans and Italians who helped build the city to the Quakers, Mormons, Unitarians, Millerites, Shakers and Pentecostals who made it a part of the Psychic Highway. It drew not only free blacks, like Douglass, who practiced root traditions and challenged social conventions, but anti-Freemasons, abolitionists, feminists, activists, reformers, outsiders and others, time and again, including those engaged, as the nineteenth century wore on, in the fierce political and social battles that would give way to the Civil War. This collection of radicals and the open minded allowed a new religion, spiritualism, to find a home in Rochester as well.

In the same way that natural hoodoos are a collection of layers deposited over time, the legend of Hoodoo Corner is the layering of memories about the famous, infamous and not-so-famous people. They are the visionaries and their visions that contributed to the story of Rochester and America— Handsome Lake, Ebenezer Allen, Nathaniel Rochester, Erastus Granger, Dewitt Clinton, Charles Finney, William Morgan, Thurlow Weed, William Lyman, Octavius Barron, Joseph Smith, Frederick Douglass, Maggie and Kate Fox, William Bloss, Mathias the Hoodoo Doctor, Victor Gruen and, of course, John C. McCurdy—and became the unlikely catalysts for America's great social movements, leaving a little something of themselves behind in the process.

# APPENDIX
# Hoodoo Corner Timeline

### Millions of Years Ago

The Ice Age begins, covering Rochester with ice two miles thick. In the ensuing thousands of years, the ice recedes, leaving in its wake geologic formations known variously as tent rocks, earth pyramids, fairy chimneys and hoodoos.

### 1300

The Seneca begin to inhabit the region and construct walking trails. One of these trails becomes East Avenue, ending near Main and Elm Streets. An ancient Indian burial site is found there, designated with a pile of stones. These formations are sometimes referred to as hoodoos.

### 1824

Erastus Granger builds the Farmers' Tavern and Inn, located on the corner of Main and Elm Streets. In the hotel's seventy-year history before being torn down in 1893 to make way for a department store, there were stories of suicide and murder, including one of a ghost that wandered its halls.

# Appendix

## 1901

John C. McCurdy arrives from Philadelphia and purchases the store located on Main and Elm. At the time, McCurdy is warned by area merchants that the location is believed to be cursed and known as Hoodoo Corner. Undaunted, McCurdy's Department Store is established.

## 1962

Midtown Plaza is constructed, becoming the nation's first urban indoor shopping mall. The size of the complex is eighteen acres and includes McCurdy's Department Store.

## 1994–2010

McCurdy's is sold to the May Company in 1994 and subsequently ceases business activities. Midtown Plaza shutters its doors in 2008 after years of decline. The location of Main and Elm Streets, once an active and vital location for Rochester commerce, now lies empty.

# Notes

## 1. Hoodoo Corner

1. M. Jeffrey Hardwick, *Mall Maker: Victor Gruen, Architect of the American Dream* (Philadelphia: University of Pennsylvania Press, 2004), 20–22, passim.
2. J. Forbes, "The Case for Urban Planning," *Urban Studies* 3, no. 2 (June 1966), 175–76.
3. Malcolm Gladwell, "Terrazo Jungle," *New Yorker Magazine* (March 15, 2004).

## 2. Masters of the Crossroads

4. "J.C. McCurdy, Department Store Founder, Dies at 81 After Illness of Four Years," *Democrat Chronicle*, January 27, 1934.

## 3. Hoodoo

5. He should not be confused with the more famous Ebenezer Allan (1743–1806) of Massachusetts and Vermont, who belonged to the politically prominent clan that also produced his second cousin, Ethan.
6. Donovan A. Shilling, "Rochester's Romantic Rogue: The Life and Times of Ebenezer Allan," *Crooked Lake Review*, http://www.crookedlakereview.com/articles/136_167/136summer2005/136shilling.html.
7. "Interesting Info," Rochester History Alive, http://www.rochesterhistoryalive.com/interesting_facts.htm.

## 4. The Code of Handsome Lake

8. Bruce E. Johansen, *The Forgotten Founders: How the American Indian Shaped Democracy* (Boston, MA: Harvard Common Press, 1982).

## 5. The Psychic Highway

9. Peter L. Bernstein, *Wedding of the Waters: The Erie Canal and the Making of a Great Nation* (New York: W.W. Norton Co., 2005), 381.
10. The Erie Canal, http://www.eriecanal.org/.
11. Elise Lathrop, *Early American Taverns and Inns* (New York: Lathrop Press, 2007), 252.
12. Lynne Belluscio, "Ganson Tavern," *LeRoy Pennysaver & News*, http://www.leroypennysavernews.com/LynneBelluscioArticles/Ganson_Tavern.htm.

## 6. The Strange Disappearance of Captain William Morgan

13. William Morgan, *Illustrations of Masonry by One of the Fraternity*, http://www.utlm.org/onlinebooks/captmorgansfreemasonrycontents.htm.
14. John Daniel, "Two Faces of Freemasonry," Biblioteca Pleyades, http://www.bibliotecapleyades.net/sociopolitica/sociopol_masonsknightstemplar03.htm.
15. Robert Morris, *William Morgan or Political Anti-Masonry: Its Rise, Growth and Decadence* (New York: Robert Macoy, Masonic Publisher, 1883), 121.
16. W.J. Chaplin, ed., *Michigan Freemason: A Monthly Magazine Devoted to Masonic and Home Literature* 7 (1876), 121.
17. Masonic Alert.com, http://www.masonicalert.com/antimasonicparty.htm.
18. Allison D. Bryant, "The Morgan Affair: What Happened to Morgan," Grand Lodge of British Columbia and Yukon, http://freemasonry.bcy.ca/texts/morgan_theory.html.
19. "The Confessions," Grand Lodge of British Columbia and Yukon, http://www.freemasonry.bcy.ca/anti-masonry/morgan_confessions.html.
20. "William Morgan's Bones: A Skeleton in a Quarry in Genesee County," *New York Times*, July 22, 1881.

## 7. Root Work

21. Emerson Klees, *The Crucible of Ferment: New York's Psychic Highway* (Rochester, N.Y.: Cameo Press, 2001).
22. "Chapter 2," *Memoirs of Rev. Charles G. Finney* (New York: A.S. Barnes and Company, 1876).
23. Ibid.
24. Mitch Horowitz, *Occult America: The Secret History of How Mysticism Shaped Our Nation* (New York: Penguin Press, 2009).
25. "The Expositor Office," LDS-mormon.com, http://www.lds-mormon.com/06.shtml.
26. Ibid.
27. Winthrop S. Hudson, *Religion in America* (New York: Charles Scribner & Sons, n.d.).
28. "Our Early History," First Baptist Church, Rochester, http://www.fbcrochester.net/history.html.
29. C. Peter Ripley, *The Black Abolitionist Papers: The United States, 1830–1846* (Chapel Hill: University of North Carolina Press, 1991), 331, passim.
30. "The Second Baptist Church congregation voted to provide seating for 'black Americans' sometime between 1840 and 1842. Many of our early records were lost in the meeting house fire of 1859, so a precise date is unknown." Arlen G. Vernava, pastor of the Baptist Temple in Rochester, New York, interview with the author, June 17, 2010.
31. "About Us," the Baptist Temple, http://www.baptempl.org/aboutus.html.

## 8. The Murder of William Lyman

32. Testimony taken from original court transcript and "Outrage Unparallelled in Rochester—Assassination!" *Daily Advertiser*, October 30, 1837.

## 9. Hoodoo Doctor

33. Norman Coombs, "History of African Americans in Rochester, NY," RIT, http://people.rit.edu/nrcgsh/arts/rochester.htm.
34. Bill Casselman, "Hoodoo," BillCasselman.com, http://www.billcasselman.com/casselmania/hoodoo.htm.
35. Henry Hyatt, *Hoodoo, Conjuration, Witchcraft, Rootwork*, vol. 2 (New York: Harper Books, 1926), 1,761. Hyatt, an Episcopal priest, collected more than 5,000 pages of transcribed testimony on these subjects in the 1930s.

His work is housed in the UCLA Center for the Comparative Study of Folklore and Mythology.
36. Margo Jefferson, "The 2 Faces of Ebonics: Disguise and Superiority," *New York Times*, January 7, 1997.
37. Samuel C. Taylor, "A Hoodoo Doctor," Manuscript Collection, William L. Clements Library, University of Michigan, Ann Arbor, Michigan, 77–80.
38. Frederick Douglass, *The Narrative of the Life of Frederick Douglass* (self published, 1845).
39. David Brown, *Conjure/Doctors: An Exploration of a Black Discourse in America, Antebellum to 1940* (New York: Columbia University Press, 1990).
40. Frederick Douglass, "The Hypocrisy of American Slavery, July 4, 1852," Fordham University, http://www.fordham.edu/halsall/mod/douglass-hypo.html.
41. "John Brown and the Harpers Ferry Raid," West Virginia Division of Culture and History, http://www.wvculture.org/history/jnobrown.html.

## 10. THE STRANGE AND TRAGIC LIVES OF THE FOX SISTERS

42. Ann Braude, *Radical Spirits: Spiritualism and Women's Rights in Nineteenth Century America* (Boston, MA: Beacon Press, 1989), 2.
43. John Mullholland, *Beware Familiar Spirits (Perspectives in Psychical Research)* (New York: Arno Press, 1938), 43.
44. Rebecca Loncraine, *The Real Wizard of Oz: The Life and Times of L. Frank Baum* (New York: Gotham, 2009).
45. "Bones in 'Old Spook House," *New York Times*, November 23, 1904.
46. *Boston Journal*, November 23, 1904.
47. Joe Nickell, "A Skeleton's Tale: The Origins of Modern Spiritualism," the Committee for Skeptical Inquiry, http://www.csicop.org/si/show/skeletons_tale_the_origins_of_modern_spiritualism/. A web site run by a modern debunker, he has many of the sources and examined much of the evidence around the discovery and provenance of the bones.

## CONCLUSION

48. Rochester Public Art, http://www.rochesterpublicart.com/public_art/?art=liberty_pole.
49. "WhatIs(a)Hoodoo?" Flickr, http://www.flickr.com/photos/25679342@N00/2670678349/.
50. Casselman, "Hoodoo."

# About the Author

Michael Keene worked for twenty-five years in the financial services industry as a financial planner. He also is the award-winning producer of *Visions, True Stories of Spiritualism, Secret Societies & Murder*, which in part inspired this book. He lives in Pittsford, New York, with his wife, Diana, and their daughter, Michele, and grandson, Joshua. His website address is http://www.ad-hoc-productions.com and e-mail is info@ad-hoc-visions.com.

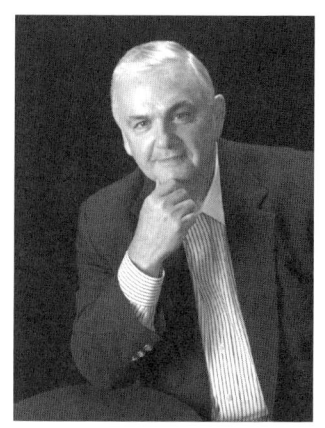

Visit us at
www.historypress.net